TIME GONE Volume 2 (More Wisdom For Living)

By Jack Alan Levine

Published by Great Hope Publishing LLC, Windermere, Florida

Cover Design & Layout by Scott Wolf

www.JackAlanLevine.com

Email: Jack@JackAlanLevine.com

Copyright 2025 Jack Alan Levine. All rights reserved. Printed in the United States of America. Excerpt as permitted under the United States Copyright Act of 1976, no part of this publication may be reproduced or distributed in any form, or by any means, or stored in a database retrieval system, without the prior written permission of the copyright holder, except by a reviewer, who may quote brief passages in review. Neither the Publisher nor the author is engaged in rendering advice or services to the individual reader. Neither the authors nor the publisher shall be liable or responsible for any loss, injury, or damage allegedly arising from any information or suggestion in this book. The opinions expressed in this book represent the personal views of the author and not of the publisher, and are for informational purposes only.

Many of the various stories of people in this book draw from real-life experience, at certain points involving a composite of stories. In some instances, people's names have been changed in the stories to protect privacy.

ISBN NUMBER 978-1-7356075-1-1 (PAPERBACK)

LIBRARY OF CONGRESS NUMBER 2025946659

TIME GONE

VOLUME 2
MORE WISDOM
FOR LIVING

INTRODUCTION

People ask where has all the time gone? Well fortunately I don't have to wonder. The answer is in these pages. Years ago, I published "TIME GONE: Wisdom For Living" which was an accumulation of the best thoughts, experiences and ideas that I shared with many family and friends in an annual holiday letter.

Well a decade has gone by since that publication and since then I have compiled 10 more years worth of new insight, deep inner thoughts and experiences. As time rolls by and history continues to record it, I wanted to share with you these new thoughts. I believe they have value, and can and will give you insight and understanding into life and happiness. I hope they provide encouragement and inspiration to live your best life, be your best self, be who you want to be and to enjoy the days and time you have.

I truly believe this book will be a blessing to you. That is my hope. If I've missed anything or you have an idea to share with me, I'd love to hear from you.

In the meantime, keep the train rolling and TO GOD BE THE GLORY!

Jack

DEDICATION

I dedicate this book to all my family and friends who walked with me through the years. Some all my life and some for a season here or there. I so much appreciate the privilege of knowing you, sharing life's ups and downs… hopefully mostly ups! I pray I have been on the giving end of a lot of love and laughter as I know I have received much of that from all of you.

I usually individually by name thank my wife, my children, my parents, brother, sister-in-law, uncles, aunts and cousins and close friends. This time I am giving a collective shout out to all of them and would like to include everyone else… those of you who I have stood behind on line at the grocery or sat next to at a coffee shop. Those of you who've been kind enough to give me a wave or smile or those who let me share a life experience or thought that comes to my mind. Even those who have cut me off with your cars when I was driving… smile! Whether you are a stranger, a new friend I met at a conference or church or at a party or Springsteen concert or ballgame or anywhere else in this wonderful life that we have journeyed together, this book is for you.

I dedicate this book collectively to all of you and personally to each of you. I know every person has a heart and mind and I pray that yours are filled with happiness and joy, excitement and contentment and you are full of love, laughter and life shining as a bright light to the world.

I've had so many wonderful moments in my life and most of them has been as a result of an interaction with people. Clearly for me as a man of God, the most amazing interaction I have ever had and value the most is my personal relationship with Jesus Christ, my Lord and Savior. That is an indescribable one that you have to experience for yourself to understand. I hope you do. Regardless, I send you my love and I hope wisdom, knowledge and experience that will benefit and bless you.

So I dedicate this book to you who hold it in your hands (or seeing it on your screen or listening to an audio version) because now there's no question after you read this book we will know each other. You will probably know me a little better than I know you… but hey you got to start somewhere… Smile! All my love.

Jack

December 2016

FAMILY UPDATE

Greetings from Orlando. It is difficult for us to believe we've been here for over a year now. The move has been a phenomenal one for us. Beth, the kids and I love it and can feel God's hand all over it. He has established us here in the community, given us an amazing church to be a part of and grow with, and given us friends and a host of other opportunities both personal and professional. We are blessed.

Those of you who received our letter last year know we stepped out in faith to answer God's call, as He closed a thirty-year chapter in our life in South Florida and called us to move to Orlando not knowing what the future held. By far, the best move we ever made was stepping out in faith and trusting God. I truly cannot imagine what life would be like had we not moved to Orlando. We are so grateful to God for his blessing, but also the great reminder for all of us this holiday season that it's imperative we seek God, and not only that we seek Him, but we hear His voice when he speaks to our hearts through His Holy Spirit. Even more importantly is that we follow what He calls us to do. God doesn't need us to follow Him; He wants us to follow Him so He can bless us and shower His grace and mercy on us, so we may fulfill the plan He has for our life and receive the blessings of walking with Him through life and, of course, the blessing in eternity of living a life faithful to God. Notice of course I didn't say a perfect life, just one loving and faithful to God.

I did get to see Bruce Springsteen in Pittsburgh this year, always a treat for me. His live shows never get old, they just keep getting better. Bruce's autobiography came out this year, he talked about his own personal lifelong struggle with depression as a result of family genetics and history. Just a reminder to all of us that many physical, emotional and spiritual issues in life cut across every demographic, geographic and psychographic profile. So if you are happy this holiday season, count it as a blessing. Bruce is a man who has everything by the world standards, except peace in his own heart and mind. I would say that peace, joy and happiness are truly what makes a person rich!

Through all of this I want to remind you that God is the most important thing in our lives. I love Proverbs 10:22, "the Lord makes one rich and he adds no sorrow to it." I've taken that to heart, along with Proverb 19:8, "he who gets wisdom loves his own soul." It's so critical to remember that we are to love ourselves and revel and rejoice in who God created us to be.

THE TRUTH ABOUT LIFE AND DEATH

Okay a few more things. A friend of mine I knew for many years was an outstanding man, a Jewish man with a kind and wonderful heart. I knew him professionally at first but over the years we became friends. We had talks where he inquired about my faith and my relationship with God. He was definitely curious and searching and had his own set of questions for God. I would remind him that we are not God, and "God's ways are higher than ours", and that "now we know in part then we'll know in full". I completely respected and admired the fact that he was searching and wrestling with God. He was a lawyer by trade and so his nature was to be inquisitive and investigative and look for facts. I had seen him just a few months ago when I went to make changes to my will because we had purchased a new home. He was in great spirits and talked about continuing to travel the world as he always had with his wife and about the many projects and exciting things he was working on. As usual it was wonderful to see him. A few short weeks later he was dying of cancer and he was in hospice. Thanksgiving morning at 7am I went to the hospice in Boca Raton to see him. I have been to hospice before to visit other people and say goodbye and share God's love with them and my love for them. And yet as I walked into see my friend, this time I had a little bit of a different experience.

He was laying there in bed unable to communicate verbally with me but moaning and groaning (I assumed from the effects of the painkilling drugs) he was quote "out of it". But as I started to talk to him about life, as I started to thank him for being the wonderful, kind, loving, caring person he was and I started to remind him how much God loves him and about his place in eternity that God had prepared for him, I noticed when I said something that seemed to hit his heart he would moan louder and in a different voice. Of course, my hope and prayer is that as I shared Jesus love with him he accepted Jesus Christ and he is and will be, in heaven for all eternity. But the important reason I share this with you is; as I was looking down at him and realized of course that his life was going to end very, very soon, that there was no turning back, that in essence it was over for him.

I couldn't help but think about all the things he had done in his life. Those I know about and those that I didn't. I couldn't help but wonder about what he had worried about prior to finding out his aggressive cancer was going to take his life. The things he was concerned about, what bothered him, what got him angry, how he spent his time.

For me the dramatic realization this was the end of his life made me take a look at my own life, and realize of course, I was going to come to that day too at some point and so will you. And at that point, just like with my buddy, all the things that we worried about, concerned ourselves about, fretted about, got upset about, will they really have mattered? Is that how we really want to spend this precious time that we have on earth. I think not. I think we want to follow God's instruction to "be joyful always" to "leap and rejoice", to shout, to dance, to sing and of course that doesn't mean there's not trials and tribulations. We know the "rain falls on the just and the unjust". We know we suffer trials and tribulations as we go through this world. We are reminded as we go through them that God is using us for his glory, as his representative, that we will be with him for eternity in heaven when our time on earth is done, that our blessings will be based on our obedience and faith and we can expect excitedly that God will bless us "abundantly and exceedingly more than we can ask or imagine" on earth and in heaven, as we love him faithfully, with all our heart, soul and mind.

So, it was a stark reality, a shock for me, as I saw my buddy's life coming to an immediate end. It made me determined and more focused than ever to make the most of every moment. Knowing that my body, my mind and heart will all fail me at certain times and certain days and of course there will be things that get me upset and mad and frustrated. I can't control those things from happening or those emotions from coming upon me but I can control my response to them when they're happening. I don't have to let them get the best of me. I don't have to engage them and let them ruin my life and take away from the joy that I have. Of course, as always you know it's perspective... we can't change many of the circumstances and situations in our life but we can change how we look at them and how we feel about them.

I believe when you know your purpose in life, when you know your eternal destination with God, it's easy to be joyful and to follow God's instructions and love this gift of life God has given us, each and every wonderful minute of it. That's my Christmas wish and holiday wish for you as you enter the new year, that above all, you would have the peace and joy of the Lord in you and with you as you walk through this life and the certainty of your place in heaven for all eternity when your physical life on earth is over. There is nothing I know that is more valuable and that is why I keep telling you about it. In the hopes that you too will realize the truth of God in this matter and if you are not sure I encourage you to pray and seek God's face about this matter and ask him what he would have you do.

Remember this "you don't become faithful in order to be loved by God and be free… you are already free and loved by God and that's why it's possible to be faithful"!

THE TRUTH ABOUT WHAT MATTERS!

I was reading recently in the Old Testament in Numbers Chapter 25. God is speaking to Moses and he talks about Phineas, Erin's grandson and here's what he says:

Then the Lord spoke to Moses, saying: "Phinehas the son of Eleazar, the son of Aaron the priest, has turned back My wrath from the children of Israel, because he was zealous with My zeal among them, so that I did not consume the children of Israel in My zeal. Therefore say, 'Behold, I give to him My covenant of peace; and it shall be to him and his descendants after him a covenant of an everlasting priesthood, because he was zealous for his God, and made atonement for the children of Israel.'"

This blew me away as I was reading it. Get this right. God blessed Phineas because he had zeal for the things of God. He was living his life focused on God and what mattered to God and he was "zealous" for God. Which means passionate for those things of God as they were a priority in his life and God blessed him and his children because of it. I looked at my own life and I had to ask myself this question. Am I zealous for God? I believe it's a question you should ask yourself this holiday season as well. And if we are not, we need to ask ourselves why not? Have we become so overtaken and influenced and enveloped in the things of this world that we have cast aside, or put to the side, or are not focused on the things of God. Thus believing with our actions, no matter what we say with our mouths, that these things are more valuable than God. That they mean more, that they more of a blessing and benefit to us than the things of God. Oh I pray this holiday season that you and I would refocus, that we would examine our lives and ask are we zealous for God? I pray that we would turn back in repentance to God and say, "lord if I haven't been zealous, please would you make me zealous again! Lord align my heart with your heart. Let my life be focused on the things of the kingdom. Let me see the world through your eyes Lord and let what matters to you matter to me". I know of no better way to live life. I don't want to miss the blessings that God has in store for me. I know God loves me no matter what I do but I don't want to miss his blessings both on earth and in heaven.

I want to be that man after God's heart. David was far from perfect in his actions you know he slept with Bathsheba and fell short in other areas of his life, but he was zealous for the things of God and God blessed him. This is our turn in history. Our turn to live our lives zealous for God. And we can rest assured that we will get the same blessings as those before us and those after us who are zealous for the Lord. I pray that you would not be deceived by Satan, that you would not be deceived by your own flesh, that you would focus on the things of the spirit and the kingdom of God and that your attention, attitudes, heart and actions would reflect somebody who is zealous for God. You can rest assure that is the best investment you can ever make on earth and in eternity. Of that I am certain... to God be the glory.

And then I was reading in Deuteronomy chapter 30 verses 1 through 10 "Now it shall come to pass, when all these things come upon you, the blessing and the curse which I have set before you, and you call them to mind among all the nations where the Lord your God drives you, and you return to the Lord your God and obey His voice, according to all that I command you today, you and your children, with all your heart and with all your soul, that the Lord your God will bring you back from captivity, and have compassion on you, and gather you again from all the nations where the Lord your God has scattered you. If any of you are driven out to the farthest parts under heaven, from there the Lord your God will gather you, and from there He will bring you. Then the Lord your God will bring you to the land which your fathers possessed, and you shall possess it. He will prosper you and multiply you more than your fathers".

This is so great! God promises that if we return to him with all our heart, he will bring us back from captivity and have compassion on us. He promises if any were driven out, which means if they were separated and apart from

God, that God will gather us from the farthest reaches of where we are and bring us back to himself. He will bring us to the land which he possessed, which is to the spirit of God himself, and we will possess it! He will prosper us and multiply us even more than he did our father's and he will circumcise our hearts to love the Lord with all our heart and with all our soul, that we may live! What a blessing from God. His promise still applies to every person today, both Jew and Gentile. All his children, no matter where you are and how far away from God you are, you can be turned back to God.

It's like the parable of the prodigal son, as God will receive you with joy and bring you back and have compassion on you. He will fill you. He will give you all the blessings that are yours, and he does this so that you may live both a life abundant here on earth and a life eternal. I pray you would take these verses to heart, read them and that the Holy Spirit of God would speak directly to your soul about areas in your life that you need to turn back to God and I pray that you would do that and not miss Gods blessings!

Hey it's been 25 years since Jesus came into my heart. I never forget that day March 10, 1991 when he knocked on my heart and I responded. You know I say year in your out "my life has gotten better every day since then" thank you God. And looking back, I see God working in my life earlier then that. God was always there for me, it just took me a while to respond. The same is true for you. God is here for you. He's just waiting for you to respond.

It's holiday time, the world is focused on shopping and gift giving and singing songs and making merry, but this holiday season I am focused on God and I pray you are too. Not that you should miss out or eliminate all that other stuff... it's fine... enjoy it! But don't miss the main thing. And that's God. For the believer, we get to walk through this life on earth with God every single step of the way as God promises "I am with you always. I will never leave you or forsake you." We often look to the world to satisfy us. Jobs, money, relationships, health, appearance, power, prestige, all these things that are temporary, that satisfy for but a little while at most and always leave us feeling empty and unfulfilled. Then there's the love of the Lord. The one who loves us most. As every parent knows how much they love their children, that gives us a glimpse of how much God loves us. Then there is God who fills us with his love abundantly, whose joy will overflow through us, who only desires to bless us and walk with us and love us. Who is by far the greatest gift we have ever received and the gift that continues to give and give and give. His one sacrifice for all, of his Son on the cross, assured us our entry into heaven forever and his Holy Spirit inside of us assures us he is with us. Always a counselor, guiding us, teaching us and loving us each and every moment of our lives

Thank you God for the wonderful gift of life you've given us. I pray for all my brothers and sisters reading this, our friends and family who have blessed us over the years with their friendship and love, that somehow we may have been a blessing to them as well. I know every year we keep hammering home God, God, God, God! And I pray that no one ever would tire of it. I pray that I would never tire of it but that I would just continue to be joyful, joyful, joyful at the blessing, blessing, blessing we have received. How lucky we are to be children of the most high. To know for certain that God is with us, that he loves us, that our place in heaven is assured, that we are strangers passing through earth as our citizenship is in heaven. Here to glorify God, to represent the kingdom of God to those on earth. May God's light shine through you. May the world see the love of God in your heart and through your actions in your life, for there is no greater purpose and no other mission for the child of

God. May you fellowship with God and know him and communicate with him and live your life walking with him through this earth, for there is no greater blessing for the child of God then to walk hand-in-hand with God through this life remembering the desire of the Lord, and the reason he created us, was for fellowship with him. Don't miss that blessing.

THE TRUTH ABOUT REALITY OF LIFE
(Till Death Do Us Part Truth)

We continue to lift my mom up in prayer as she is burdened by the stress of caring for my dad on a day-to-day basis as his dementia has worsened over the last couple of years. And yet he is still so sweet and loving, certainly aware that his faculties aren't what they once were and frustrated by that, but still the sweetest, kindest, most wonderful man. It is our privilege now to care for him as he cared for us. Yet it is my mother who bears the brunt of the burden on a day-to-day basis even with live-in help. The emotional pressure, stress and change of life is a brutal one. We know many others are going through the same with their spouses and loved ones with dementia and Alzheimer's, many others are watching loved one suffer from cancer and other physical illnesses. Many others see their loved ones and spouses struggling with addiction, some with depression and some with physical infirmities. The underlying theme of it all is our physical bodies will fail us, that is not who we are. We are who we are in our spirit, in our hearts and our souls. Our actions reflect our spirit, hearts and minds. And I would hope and pray that in your life, that your love would overflow towards those you meet and their love would overflow towards you. And I pray that we would be patient, kind and loving to all those who are suffering physically, emotionally, spiritually and financially in any way shape or form.

Everybody needs love! Everybody. As Bob Dylan said "love is all there is, it makes the world go round, love and only love, it can't be denied, no matter what you think about it, you won't be able to do without it, take a tip from one who's tried." You got that one right Bobby. The last word of wisdom I can share with you is the only love that is unbreakable, that you cannot lose, that will never withdraw itself from you no matter what you do, is the everlasting, undeniable, unbelievable, incomprehensible, undeserved love of God, that God himself has showered on us to from heaven through the death of his son Jesus on the cross and by placing his Holy Spirit inside of our heart, as a deposit and confirmation of his love and our place in heaven. Thank you Jesus!

THE TRUTH ABOUT TIME/TIME MACHINES

"You can't go back – but you were there!"

I want to share with you a few things that have happened to me lately and a couple of thoughts I had. I found some old reel to reel tapes that I made from 1975 to 1984. Back then I just turned on the reel to reel and hit record as I was playing my guitar and singing. I had 20 reel to reel tapes laying around in a box that had been sitting in my closet for all these years. Of course the reel to reel is pretty obsolete but I had the opportunity to have them converted to CDs. Over the course of a month driving in my car I listened to these CDs. It was truly like being in a time machine, like being able to go back to the past, almost ghost-like, revisiting a portion of my life that I had previously lived.

Many times when I was recording I would comment about the date and time and what was happening in my life, some of it good, some of it not so good. Sometimes a few friends would come over to play with me, old girlfriends singing songs with me on the tape, old friends teaching me licks on the guitar, me coming up with original lyrics and writing songs. I write this not to tell you that any of it was any good or noteworthy from a musical standpoint. That's not why did it. I never had any misgivings that I was to be a rock and roll star. I just enjoyed it.

Most of the time it was me alone. As I got to sit back and listen to what I was thinking and how I was feeling, some of the hurt and pain of breakups, the joy and excitement of life going well, graduating college, friends, new jobs on Madison Avenue, happy times. There was one quote from 1982 where I said "I've never been happier in all my life". How great was that... hearing those tapes was truly for me as if I'd seen a ghost and it was great. I enjoyed it so much. There was some events and occurrences that I never would have remembered. It was so awesome to get to listen back on some of the thoughts, concepts, ideas, insanity and laughter that was going on in those days... and yes, some of it was fueled by too much marijuana smoking... but nonetheless those were college days and a few years after. It was recorded, this time capsule of almost a decade of audio recordings. By the way had I been able to listen to the recordings back then I probably could've improved my guitar playing and singing a little bit, but that's a whole other story.

I was truly fascinated by the ability to go back and have a glimpse into my life. It sent chills up my spine and excited me. The original songs I had written reflected well on what I was going through in my life. But more interesting and fascinating to me were the comments I'd make before the songs, which gave me a true glimpse into how I was feeling and what I was thinking. Very, very, glad I got to do this. So why am I telling you all this...?

BECAUSE THE TRUTH IS LIFE IS A PARADE

A few weeks ago, I went to downtown Winter Garden at 9am in the morning to line up for the town's annual Christmas parade. You know the drill ...Fire Chief, politicians, floats, marching bands and a variety of other businesses and organizations representing the town lines up from one end of the street to the other. These parades take place in towns all across America usually on July 4 and of course on Christmas.

Winter Garden is not a small town so the parade lined up for at least 20 blocks and ended in the heart of downtown, where I stood waiting for the parade to come by. My only motive for being in the parade was to see my daughter Talia who's dance company was marching in the 2 1/2 mile parade. Beth was not feeling well that morning and of course I did not want to miss Talia dancing so I went. As I was waiting for the parade to come my way I couldn't help but notice all the people lined up. Americana I thought. This is the heart of America. This is the heart of life. Look at all these people. Young, old, many with families and young kids excited about the parade.

Most of the kids were excited because it was a known fact that most of the floats and cars and trucks and organizations that came by would dole out candy all along the way to the kids lined up in the streets…for the kids it was a candy bonanza. But for me as I looked around the streets lined up with people, it dawned on me that this was life that everywhere in America, all through towns in the USA people were lining up and doing the same thing on this day, or this weekend or next weekend, but in fact everybody was having the same experience, or at least everybody who wanted to. And it dawned on me how we very much live the same lives. That whether I'm in Winter Garden Florida, Syracuse New York, Peoria Illinois or San Diego California... pretty much in every town, village and city throughout the country parades will happen, people lining up, people living life just being Americans. And it dawned on me how much our lives are the same and how much we go through the same experiences in life. But of course each one of us is unique, created by God with the unique fingerprint, heartbeat and mind that only belongs to us.

So it made sense to me and I got clarity and inspiration and revelation from God. God's message to me was this: yes, in theory people do the same things and live the same lives. So, if that's the case then you need to enjoy your unique life as much as you can. You need to embrace it, indulge it, let it envelop you and live it to the fullest. Because it's the only one you get here on earth. We work, we go on vacations, we watch our kids grow up and then our grand kids and we go from event to event, from concert to movie to comedy club to sporting event to bowling league to softball league to card game to fishing hole to hunting outing or to a vacation to Paris or to the mountains of Tennessee. Maybe we make it out to Vegas for a trade show or we buy a new car. We buy a house, we upsize, then downsize. We buy new clothes, they go out of style so we buy more new clothes. We buy the latest electronic equipment... first color TVs, then big-screen plasmas, now HD, cell phones, computers, iPads all the cool games and toys of our lifetime. We root and cheer for our sports teams.

We yell and scream over politics and religion and right and wrong and good and bad and we live our nights and days as we wake up to the morning light and go to bed to the evening darkness and repeat the same procedure day in day until our time on earth is up. That is the context of our lives. But that is not our lives!!! Our lives are the moments we make it! Our lives are the joy we bring to it and to others. Yes, our lives are within the confines of that time and circumstances we are all given... but it's our job to make the most of it! It's not about how long you live it's about how you live the time you have! And it's not a bad thing that basically we all do the same stuff, obviously with some variation, it's actually a good thing... there's nothing wrong with that.

Imagine if you will, everybody in the world taking a road trip from Florida to California. Everybody did the same thing but not everybody had the same experience. What did you do on your car trip? were you laughing, singing, telling stories and playing games... joyful as you appreciate the time you had with the other passengers in the car, your family or friends. Or were you miserable and upset. Was the trip a burden and you were just angry and frustrated the whole time and enjoyed none of it. That my friends is our lives and our choice!!!

On this journey. On this trip, we get to decide the circumstances and dictate our happiness. I believe our happiness is something we choose and is ingrained in us regardless of the circumstances. So while a great concert, a winning sports event, a championship team, a new job, a new relationship, making a lot of money, a wedding, a child's birth, the graduations are all certainly highlights that we can mark the road of our journey in time with... yet they are not what life is about! Life is about what we did during the time and ride of your life.

Two people are given a pass to Disneyland they both go to the park. They both ride the same rides but they both didn't have the same experience. The one who went in happy and childlike and excited and not worried about when the park closes or how crowded it was, but just enjoyed each and every ride as if they were seeing it for the first time... they had the greatest day ever. The one whining and grumbling about the price of admission, about the length of time they had to wait on line to get on the rides, about how hot it was ...they didn't enjoy any of it! And this again my friends is our life!

God gave us life to enjoy, as a child experiencing stuff for the first time and even though we may repeat the same behavior, even though we may go to the same parades every year and see the same people and do some of the same things... the gift, the joy, the wonder, is in being alive to experience this day and hopefully the next day. I know many wealthy people who have all the resources of the world at their hands who are the most miserable people I know. I also know many people who are definitely living in poverty who are living the most joyful, fulfilled, happy lives you have ever seen. It all has to do with their attitude and with their gratitude for being alive. With their joy and lust and zeal for living. I hope and pray this holiday season that you would be filled with joy and lust and zeal for living unlike anything you've ever experienced before...not concerned about the circumstances of your life. Where you live, the size of your bank account or apartment/house, but that you would look at each new day is an opportunity to live, think, give, share, love, laugh and spend another day alive, another day that you never had before... a new day...another gift from God.

2016

THE TRUTH ABOUT STOCK MARKET REALLY REFLECTING LIFE

Last year's holiday letter, for the first time ever (and I probably won't ever do it again) included the stocks I was taking positions in at the end of the year. I gave you a list of them as I felt that market valuations were way off. I also made it a point to tell you do not ask me when to sell the stocks. Well we had a total gain of 64.8% on 12 picks.

Obviously you can see I made some good choices. These choices don't always work out. Sometimes our timing is off and sometimes we are just wrong, which is why it's always important to be diversified in your stock portfolio, so if you're wrong in one situation you are not wiped out. That is a timeless investing lesson and one my dad drilled into my head. Thank you Dad, for that lesson and many others that have saved me a lot of aggravation and blessed me abundantly and made me appear much smarter than I am simply by following the wisdom that you had lived by.

Anyway the point is that we should know the value of things! And that we should know when something is overvalued or undervalued and I'm not just talking about the stock market. I'm talking about cars, artwork, houses, relationships, jobs and situations. Remembering the value of things should not necessarily be determined by the world and what artificial price they put on it. For instance, if you knew that a certain iPhone was worth $400 and somebody wanted to charge you $800 you would say that's ridiculous. I'm not paying $800 it's only worth $400. Yet if they wanted to sell you that very same phone for $100 you probably would buy as many as you could. And even borrow money to buy some because you knew what the true value is. That's a great philosophy for stock market investing and real estate investing and I truly admire those people who do whatever it takes to understand what the true value of things are. Their investments are not a guess or a hope. They are based on research, study, knowledge and wisdom.

Most importantly, the reason I share this with you is you need to understand the value of your relationship with God. It is worth everything. God is worth everything you have. It is worth forsaking all for, giving all for. The return is invaluable. He is invaluable, his love is invaluable, his joy is invaluable, his peace is invaluable...and the greatest news of all is you are invaluable to him. Don't sell God short. Take everything you have and invest in God, for that is where the true treasure lies! One whose value can never be determined by the world. One whose value can never be lowered by the world, for it is safe and secure from the beginning of time, for all eternity, the Alpha and the Omega, the beginning and the end is the Lord. I love in God's word (the Bible) where it says "God is well pleased to give you the kingdom to his children". Thank you Lord.

It's important to know the value of things and invest in what you believe in and not be swayed by the world. Don't get caught up or swept up in waves of enthusiasm or waves of pessimism that the world gets involved in regarding finances, politics, morals, music, sports, clothing, trends, styles or anything. Know for yourself what is real and valuable! Don't depend on others to tell you… that is the message my friends! For me I have found the value in the kingdom of God and it is the greatest treasure of all.

THE TRUTH ABOUT BAND OF GOLD

So here's the last part of the story. I'm driving along about a month ago and the song "Band of Gold" sung by Freda Payne came into my head. Now I remember the song, as growing up in the 70s I was a teenager and that song was a big hit and was a catchy tune... "now that you're gone, all that's left is a band of gold, all that's left of the dreams I hold is a band of gold", etc. etc. I haven' thought about the song in 30 years and I don't know why that particular day it popped into my head. It did not play on the radio it just came into my mind. The artist singing the words as I remember them and the chorus which is especially catchy. So for three or four days the song was in my head and yes I was singing it loudly when I was alone in my car, then all of a sudden I opened up the newspaper in Orlando and I see that Freda Payne is coming to play a benefit concert at a local church. I say "come on God that's a little too weird". So I double checked my spirit and prayed to make sure I'm not crazy. That indeed I'm supposed to go see Freda. I have seen this happen in my life at least a dozen times over the last 25 years since I've been saved. The Holy Spirit speaks to my heart about something. It might seem insane and crazy to the world and probably is, yet I know it's something I'm supposed to do. A place I'm supposed to go or someone I'm supposed to see, or something I'm supposed to do, and I have followed it every time.

I made sure again this time and felt another confirming signal that I was supposed to be there, so I bought tickets to go. Knowing that it wasn't necessarily about seeing Freda Payne, but that there was some reason I was supposed to be there that night. It was the same night as the day I had spent at the parade Talia was dancing in. Talia now 12, came with me to the show, it was a daddy/daughter night, of course she was the youngest person there. Freda Payne sang along with Maureen McGovern and Florence LaRue (from the Fifth Dimension). Freda sang "Band of Gold" and I loved it. The music was great, the show was great and they sang some Christmas carols after which was great. Talia and I had a lot of laughs at the show. God spoke to me in a couple ways.

First, Freda sang a ballad that she dedicated to people who were 70 and over... (thank God I'm not there yet) ... but that was a reflective ballad of life and loving and living and a reminder that even though we've done so much, were far from finished yet. God spoke to me through that. Then when Freda sung "Band of Gold" she did great, but she was not able to hit the exact high notes from the song over 40 years ago. And that's when God reminded me "you can't go back"...but he spoke to my spirit again and said "BUT YOU WERE THERE!" And that's what I want to remind you of. You may not have the luxury of having recorded 20 hours of audio tape over a 10 year period or a lifetime to go back to, of course you can look at a picture and remember a particular time in your life, but perhaps not all of the details of what happened at the time. And of course you can listen to a song that had special relevance in a specific time in your life and it will take you back to a point in time, make you remember those feelings for an old girlfriend, boyfriend, or time in your life that you were extremely happy or sad. But the truth of the matter is you can't go back to that time... that's okay! Just remember... you were there! You had the experience... you lived it.

So the moral of the story is we are not to live in the past, we are to live now. And although we can't go back to the past and be with the people we were with and have the experiences we had and live those memories again, we did have them! How blessed and lucky we were to have lived those moments (especially the good ones) But we also have this great gift of today! To make a new memory. Go to lunch with a friend. Go to a new movie. Watch the game, play a game. Go fishing, go hunting, go on vacation, sing another song and go to another parade.

2016

My prayer for you and I this holiday season is that we would never tire of the repetitive things of life. That we would never bemoan the fact that "it's just another parade". No, rather we would always have that excitement of little kids. I want to go to the parade and indeed our lives should be a parade as we march through... laughing, singing, joyful, waving to the people on all sides, knowing that our actions are bringing joy to the people who are watching and getting joy ourselves from our ability to be in the parade. So you say " Jack is the end result of all this you're trying to tell me... life is a parade!" I'll go with that. And remember this... you can't go back to where you were in the parade... you only are where you're at now... but you should never have any regrets... because you were there! So live where you're living. I'll say it again... live where you're living! And remember to live before you die!! and I thank God this holiday season that for every believer in Jesus Christ that our lives on earth are just the beginning of the parade for us and we know for certain that we will be in a parade for all eternity... joyful, laughing, living, loving and we will be parading with our Savior... oh my what a day of rejoicing that will be, when we all get to heaven! Thank you God for our wonderful lives.

TIME GONE VOLUME 2

We thank you this holiday season for our wonderful friends and family God bless you all.

All of our love greetings and blessings to you this year from our family to yours.

Jack, Beth, Jackson and Talia

December 2017

TIME GONE VOLUME 2

FAMILY UPDATE

To Our Amazing And Wonderful Friends And Families, Merry Christmas & Happy Holidays!

I can't believe it has been two years since we moved up to Orlando. The greatest thing we ever did was to follow God's call and move here. Beth, the kids and I are being blessed tremendously, loving our lives here and the opportunities (personal, spiritual and professional), God has laid before us.

LIFE AND DEATH

On that note my father passed away three months ago on September 10. His health had been declining the last few years. He suffered from dementia, a previous stroke and other health issues. A few months ago, he had another stroke. From a personal perspective, realizing the quality of his life would never be close to what it was or what I believe he wanted, I personally was prepared for his death. He lived 85 wonderful years, was the best father, grandfather and husband ever, and thankfully we got to share all our lives with him. It was amazing to have a father who truly loved us with all his heart and did everything for our blessing and benefit all of his life. What a great role model of love, sacrifice and parenting. Of course, needless to say, my mother is exactly the same way, which makes my brother and I the two luckiest people in the world.

Because I had personally watched dad's mental condition deteriorate over the last five years and very rapidly this last year, I realized I could no longer have the conversations, discussion and interaction with my father that I had known all my life, where he provided me counseling, guidance, love, encouragement and inspiration.

Of course, after he got sick I still loved just being with him and conversing with him on a different level and seeing him smile at simple things. Yet I came to realize years ago that I was losing the father I had known, certainly from a mental standpoint. Thus when it was evident that dad was passing from this earth I think I was able to deal with it well, accept it and certainly believed it was a blessing for him to not be suffering mentally or physically. My spiritual belief that better things lie ahead in eternity made it easier to deal with.

But I wasn't prepared for one thing. You see I was prepared for him to die, but I wasn't prepared for him to be dead! What do I mean by that? After he died I came to miss him more and more with each passing day. I don't say that to have you feel sad or sorry for me. Please don't. I'm not sad or sorry. It's actually wonderful in an intense, loving kind of way. Because while I got to appreciate him so much while he was alive and get the benefits and blessings of his love and sacrifice on my behalf, I think I get to appreciate him more and in a different way now. Of course part of him remains alive in my heart. The interesting thing is that part doesn't diminish… rather it grows daily. So now, absurdly enough (or just justice for Dad!) I find myself listening to Dixieland jazz, Dad's favorite music; and every once in a while when I'm driving, instead of Springsteen or Dylan I am throwing Dixieland jazz into the CD player and bopping to the sounds. What a joy! It's like Dad's riding in the car with me and I can still see him loving those Dixieland sounds.

I share this with you as a reminder, my family and I are grateful for the time we had with Dad. We are not complaining to God or saying it isn't fair that he is dead. Quite the opposite. We are grateful for the time we had with him and so grateful for the father we had. I hope and pray the same would be said of you in your life. I hope and pray that you would focus on your family, your life, who you are, what you are and take a deep look at how you want to be remembered by those you love. You can still write that chapter, you can write the final scene in the movie; it's not too late. It starts with sacrificial love, God demonstrated it, Jesus demonstrated it, my parents demonstrated it. I know it does not come naturally or easily for some people; in fact it does not come naturally or easily for me. But it's something I work at daily because I know it's important and I want the benefit and result of it.

So, it makes me think more of what I can do to bless my family and friends and not what can they do to bless me. Yes, you're thinking of the old President John F. Kennedy quote (those of you old enough to remember) "Ask not what your country can do for you, but ask what you can do for your country". Whether you approach it philosophically, that way, or spiritually, as God said "Love others as you love yourself", clearly it is in giving that we receive, in emptying ourselves that we are filled! I don't how to say it any more clearly than that!

I want to have a little fun this holiday season and perhaps give you some fun as well so at the end of this letter I'm sharing with you some quotes from a few poets that I find exceptionally meaningful to life. I believe many of these quotes will touch you deep down in your soul, others will make you think, both of which is the intent.

I hope you enjoy them. As always feel free to write your own and please share them with me.

Psalm 118 says "This is the day the Lord has made, we will rejoice and be glad in it." As I was thinking and praying about that verse, I realized that "this is the day the Lord has made" is a fact, at least for those that believe in God! Clearly no believer of God would dispute that God created the world and this particular day. However, "We will rejoice and be glad in it" is a choice! A choice you and I have to make each and every day. I have resolved and determined for the last few months since God really stuck this verse on my heart that I would make that choice each and every day and I do that in the morning when I get up. I remind myself this is the day the Lord has made and I make the decision today that I will rejoice and be glad in it. This has impacted my life extremely positively and I suggest the you think about doing the same. The Apostle Paul said physical exercise is good but we need to strengthen and exercise our spiritual muscles.

I know how much my mom and dad love me. They demonstrated it to me all my life. I know how much God loves me, He demonstrated it to me since I accepted him at 33 years old in unbelievable, undeniable and yes sometimes unexplainable ways. I am so grateful to be the beneficiary of my physical parents love and my families love and of course my God's love. On that last note, just in case you're seeking the secret to life and want to have complete peace and joy by having and experiencing the fullness of God in your life...It is very simple. God showed it to me it's in Ephesians 3:15-19 Paul is praying for the church and its believers....and for me God just boiled it all down to those simple versus:

"I pray that out of his glorious riches he may strengthen you with power through his Spirit in your inner being, so that Christ may dwell in your hearts through faith. And I pray that you, being rooted and established in love, 18 may have power, together with all the Lord's holy people, to grasp how wide and long and high and deep is the love of Christ, and to know this love that surpasses knowledge—that you may be filled to the measure of all the fullness of God."

All I've ever wanted was to know and experience the fullness of God. Paul showed me exactly how to get it and that is to just comprehend how much God loves me. Thank you God! Oh, by the way, God loves you the same amount. Any of you who have kids know you love all your kids the same amount. It's not that each kid gets half your love or a portion of it. No! Each kid gets a 100% of your love. That's the amazing math of God. God loves all of us one hundred percent.

I pray you do not miss the blessing and joy of a life lived with the love of God. This ongoing relationship of walking with God, knowing God and being loved by Him daily is not far away or unreachable. God resides in our hearts if we invite Him in.

That said our family wishes your family the happiest of holidays, the greatest of years and the utmost of blessing. We pray that you rejoice in your time here on earth, that you are not fearful of the evil things of the world, but instead accept them as part of playing in the game. Like football players getting hit during the game, they prepare and train themselves for it because they know it is a part of the game. Their eyes are focused on the prize… winning! They understand that the game is a battle. So we need to have the same focus and determination, and the will and want to win the battle for the kingdom of God. We do that by glorifying God with our lives, by being light in a world of darkness and salt to tasteless generation. By being a reflection of the love, mercy, grace, principals and righteousness of God.

One last thing I want to share with you and I know this has been a very spiritual letter, I'm sure you're not surprised by that. When Jesus preached he was able to literally in 10 minutes explain everything. Some Pastors take hours (I know I do!), some take weeks, years and lifetimes trying to interpret the word of God and explain it. Theologians and scholars and teachers do the same. Yet Jesus summed it all up in 10 minutes. If you're curious what those 10 minutes are just read Matthew chapters 5,6 and 7, then you will have the entire Gospel at your fingertips. It is sometimes referred to as the "Sermon on the Mount" but it is simply a perfect explanation of the truth of God… simply, wonderfully and beautifully put.

Jesus also said man does not live on bread alone, but on every word that comes out of the mouth of God. These last few months my hunger and desire for God's Word has increased tremendously. It is hard for me to believe as I've been walking with God for 26 years now, yet it just keeps getting better and better. If you would've told me there would be such a dramatic increase in my hunger and desire for more of God's Word at this stage of my life it would've surprised me. But it seems like right now my desire for God's word is the same as when I'm starving and wanting filet mignon or a great pizza. I just can't wait to get it; I can't wait to taste it, chew it, enjoy it, swallow it and be filled by it.

That is the same feeling I have each and every day when I wake and go to chew on and feast on the Word of God. Now I understand that verse like never before. When Jesus said we live on the Word of God, as it is truly food for my spirit, soul, mind and body. I don't know if the Holy Spirit is working in me more or I am just wising up and desiring more of God. Either way it's amazing and I just want to remind you it's available to each and every one of you. It is not something you have to go to seminary to learn. You do not have to be a pastor or a rabbi or a scholar to have any of these benefits. You just have to show up and taste of the Lord and you will see that He is good!

AMAZING QUOTES TO MAKE YOU THINK THIS HOLIDAY SEASON

1. The meaning of life has been lost in the wind
   And some people thinkin' that the end is close by
   'Stead of learnin' to live they are learnin' to die.

2. But the thing that scared me most was
    When my enemy came close
    And I saw that his face looked just like mine.

3. I'll know my song well before I start singing.

4. Yet there's no one to beat you
    No one to defeat you
    'Cept the thoughts of yourself feeling bad.

5. You don't need a weatherman
    To know which way the wind blows.

6. Well, I try my best
    To be just like I am
    But everybody wants you
    To be just like them.

7. And though the rules of the road have been lodged
    It's only people's games that you've got to dodge.

8. While money doesn't talk, it swears.

9. And if my thought-dreams could be seen
    They'd probably put my head in a guillotine.

10. You never understood that it ain't no good
    You shouldn't let other people
    get your kicks for you.

11. When you got nothing, you got nothing to lose.

12. But how long, babe, can you search for what's
    not lost?

13. An' here I sit so patiently
    Waiting to find out what price
    You have to pay to get out of
    Going through all these things twice.

14. And don't go mistaking Paradise
    for that home across the road.

15. Love is all there is, it makes the world go 'round
    Love and only love, it can't be denied
    No matter what you think about it
    You just won't be able to do without it
    Take a tip from one who's tried.

16. Grandma said, "Boy, go and follow your heart
    And you'll be fine at the end of the line

2017

        All that's gold isn't meant to shine
        Don't you and your one true love ever part."

17. May you grow up to be righteous
     May you grow up to be true
     May you always know the truth
     And see the light surrounding you.

18. Time is a jet plane, it moves too fast.

19. You do what you must do and you do it well.

20. Time is an ocean but it ends at the shore
     You may not see me tomorrow.

21. There are no mistakes in life some people say
     It is true sometimes you can see it that way.

22. I finally realize there's no room for regret.

23. If you don't believe there's a price
     For this sweet paradise
     Remind me to show you the scars.

24. Well, it may be the devil or it may be the Lord
    But you're gonna have to serve somebody.

25. You either got faith or you got unbelief
    And there ain't no neutral ground.

26. The enemy is subtle, how be it we are so deceived
    When the truth's in our hearts
     and we still don't believe.

27. People starving and thirsting,
    Grain elevators are bursting
    Oh, you know it costs more to store
    the food than it do to give it.

28. When I'm gone don't wonder where I be
    Just say that I trusted in God
    and Christ was in me.

29. You harbor resentment
    You know there ain't too much of a thrill
    You wish for contentment
    But you got an emptiness that can't be filled.

30. Many try to stop me, shake me up in my mind
    Say, "Prove to me that He is Lord,
    show me a sign"
    What kind of sign they need
    When it all come from within
    When what's lost has been found,
    What's to come has already been?

31. Wherever I am welcome is where I will be.

32. When destruction cometh swiftly
    And there's no time to say fare-thee-well
    Have you decided whether you want to be
    In heaven or in hell?

33. You can play with fire but you'll get the bill.

34. I see people who are supposed to know better
    Standin' around like furniture.

35. Talk about salvation, people suddenly get tired
    They got a million things to do,
      they're all so inspired.

36. They say that patriotism is the last refuge
    To which a scoundrel clings
    Steal a little and they throw you in jail
    Steal a lot and they make you king.

37. Democracy don't rule the world
    You'd better get that in your head
    The world is ruled by violence
    But I guess that's better left unsaid.

38. And a man's gonna do what he has to do
    When he's got a hungry mouth to feed.

39. My only prayer is, if I can't be there,
    Lord, protect my child.

40. What looks large from a distance,
    Close up is never that big.

41. Someday maybe I'll remember to forget.

42. I must be guilty of something
    You just whisper it into my ear.

43. I saw thousands
     Who could have overcome the darkness
     For the love of a lousy buck
     I've watched them die.

44. Maybe someday, you will understand
     That something for nothing is everybody's plan.

45. Now I've always been the kind of person
     That doesn't like to trespass
     But sometimes you just find yourself over the line.

46. You always said people don't do
     what they believe in,
     they just do what's most convenient,
     then they repent.

47. I paid the traitor and killed him much later
     But that's just the way that I am.

48. What good am I if I'm like all the rest?
     If I just turn away, when I see how you're dressed
     If I shut myself off so I can't hear you cry
     What good am I?

49. And the cards are no good that you're holding
    Unless they're from another world.

50. Sometimes the silence can be like the thunder.

51. You always got to be prepared
    but you never know for what.

52. Someday we'll look back on this
    and it will all seem funny

53. Now everyone dreams of a love faithful and true,
    But you and I know what this world can do.
    So let's make our steps clear so the other may see
    And I'll wait for you…
    should I fall behind wait for me.

54. You can't start a fire without a spark
    You can't start a fire worrying 'bout
    your little world falling apart

55. It ain't no sin to be glad your alive

56. God have mercy on the man
    Who doubts what he's sure of

57. I'm ready to grow young again.

58. You've got to learn to live with
    what you can't rise above

59. It's a sad man my friend
    whose living in his own skin
    And can't stand the company.

60. We cannot undue these things we've done.

61. We learned more from a three-minute record
    Then we ever learned in school.

62. We made a promise
    We swore we'd always remember
    No retreat baby no surrender.

63. Leave behind your sorrows
    Let this day be the last.
    Tomorrow there'll be sunshine
    And all this darkness past

64. You shouldn't let other people
    Get your kicks for you.

65. In the field of opportunity its plowing time again.

66. He not busy being born is busy dying.

67. Don't lose hope. The future hasn't happened yet,
    Why would you view it as history?

December 2018

FAMILY UPDATE

Blessings To All Our Wonderful Family and Friends!

Thank you so much for being a part of our lives. It is amazing how often we think about you and pray for you and are grateful for you. I know we don't always talk to everybody every day but if you are getting a holiday letter it is because you have touched us at some point in our lives and we want to remain connected to you, even if it's just a once a year touch. We think it's important. Many years we think we must be crazy to go through the time and expense of getting out what in the past has been almost 800 letters a year and yet we will hear from somebody who will tell us how much the letter meant to them and impacted them. So that motivates us to sit down and write another one for yet another year. We hope it matters to you. We know the letters are long and cover a variety of topics and they are that way on purpose. We have never been about the status quo or the norm...as that's way too easy...smile!

IS YOUR LIFE A PLATFORM? IF SO FOR WHAT?

So how do you look at life? How do you look at your circumstances and your trials and tribulations? The apostle Paul saw his chains while in prison and his individual trials and tribulations as an opportunity to share the love of God and the good news of the saving gospel of Jesus Christ. How do you see your life?

I was talking to a buddy of mine yesterday who owned a pizza place and he said that the pizza place was his platform to interact with people and get to know them. He said it wouldn't matter if he was serving a slice of pizza or in the construction business selling or installing pipes. All that mattered to him was he had a platform to interact with people! How awesome is that. So whatever platform you have in your life, remember that's your opportunity to interact with people and to build relationships. The apostle Paul didn't live his life selfishly. He knew his purpose. He was called to proclaim the gospel of Jesus Christ and everything he did was to accomplish that purpose. He saw his life circumstances as his platform, as his opportunity to share and spread the good news about God...so the question this holiday season is how do you see your life?

If you are a believer in Jesus Christ I want to remind you this holiday season that there's a big difference between knowing the message and being the message! The one thing we see that summarizes the apostle Paul's life is he was sold out to God... he was the message!! I believe our lives, no matter what platform we have to live it out in, should reflect the same, and that way you would expect to be abundantly and exceedingly blessed by God more than you can ask or imagine and to hear well done good and faithful servant when you go to meet God face-to-face.

GREATEST THING I EVER HEARD!!

So I was talking to a friend of mine the other day and he commented that he would die for a stranger in a heartbeat and I thought that was an amazing comment because I don't believe that I would (for a family member yes... for a stranger, I don't think so). He's a Christian brother and he said he would die for stranger because he knows for sure he's going to heaven so he has no fear of death... And he said, what if the person who I was going to die for didn't know Jesus and isn't sure that they are going to heaven. And if I die for him and keep them alive, they still have a chance to come to know Jesus and be saved for all eternity.... that's why he would die for them he said. In my heart I was astounded. I thought to myself what great faith, what great love, what a Christlike attitude... like Jesus, this guy actually was living his life as love in its purest essence (sacrificial... putting others first). How amazing is that! It was inspiring to see somebody so sold-out for God that they were willing to follow God's word, but even more so than that, that they believed it 100% and knew for sure that they were spending heaven in eternity and that was a great place to be! I am praying and striving that God continues to mold me and shape me so that I would be more like my buddy and have a godly attitude about all things.

WHAT HAPPENS NEXT?

Paul Allen the co-founder of Microsoft died. One of the world's richest men and people had wonderful things to say about his accomplishments here on earth. But there was no mention of his eternal salvation or resting place. So here we have a man by the world standards who had everything and yet when his time was up where does he spend eternity? Where will you spend eternity? I believe it's a choice. You can choose to accept God, His love and his son Jesus sacrificial death on the cross and spend eternity with God in heaven or you can spend eternity separated from God in what we would call hell… But it is a choice. Stephen Hawking, world-famous physicist, died this year also and in his last published writing he said that "there is no God". Well one thing for certain, he knows the truth now! And I believe he now knows that he is separated from God for all eternity and that he regrets his decision and wishes he would've made different choices on this earth while he had the chance. I hope and pray that you will never have any regret about the choices you made here on earth and especially those that impact where you will spend eternity,

I WAS AN IDIOT!

I was reading in the book of Exodus the other morning in my quiet time and it was talking about how God gave the Israelites manna everyday… which was food to eat while they were in the desert. The passage was describing the manna as a wafer like substance that had a honey type taste to it and I thought that's interesting I probably could've eaten that, one of the few things I could actually eat! Smile! (that's an inside joke if you know my dietary habits/pickiness.) I had recently been praying to God about two very specific issues in my life and I was seeking God for answers to these two particular issues.

At the end of a couple of days of feverishly seeking God, God had still not answered me on these particular issues and as I read in Exodus that morning God spoke to my heart and He reminded me that my problems and concerns had nothing to do with the issues that I was requesting prayer for… but rather had to do with the condition of my heart. That the condition of my heart was not right. Because I too, was just like the Israelites. I too had not been satisfied with the manna of God I have been receiving. God reminded me "I am your joy"… And if you are not satisfied with me and my riches and joy you will never be satisfied with the things of the world… So I had to examine my own heart and realized that I had taken my focus off of God. I was asking God for certainty and security and God was asking me to trust him day by day. God has always provided abundantly for me in my life. God has always given me manna. God has always been there… it was me who would take my eyes and focus off God. It was me who would get distracted by the things of the world instead of focusing on the things of God.

So I took great joy in being refocused on God and remembering how much I love Him and how grateful I am for the life he has given me both on earth and the one to come for all eternity. I had to refocus, I had gotten distracted and off-track. I was not starving, I was not wanting and I too had begun to grumble and complain... not being satisfied with the blessing and manna that God had given, but instead desiring more of the things of the world I selfishly thought I needed or wanted. Thank you God for the great reminder.

JUST A THOUGHT FOR AMERICA!

What is happening to our world today? More importantly what is happening to America? And much more importantly what is happening to us as individuals? I have never liked this herd-like mentality, the New Year's Eve, St. Patrick's Day, Halloween, July 4th mentality... And that is not to say that I dislike the holidays themselves... quite the opposite, I'm very fond of the holidays. I don't like the fact that people use these particular days as an excuse to behave in a way that they never would otherwise. Almost like "The Purge" movie. Those of you familiar with it know the theme, there is one day where rules don't apply, there are no laws so you can kill anybody that you don't like, hence the Purge name! It seems to me people treat those holidays the same way. They just use these days as an opportunity to get rip-roaring drunk and/or to behave in a dumb or inappropriate manner and/or to just go nuts in a way they never would on any other day.

Listen if people want to get rip-roaring drunk and behave rudely or like an idiot, go ahead, but don't say that New Year's Eve or the Fourth of July or St. Patrick's Day made you do it! Just admit that's what you want to do. Why wait for a special day? It seems to me it just gives people an excuse to hide behind... it gives people a reason to behave rudely, stupidly and improperly with no regard for their neighbor, with no sense of common decency, no sense of right and wrong.

As for me, I don't need it to be Thanksgiving to give thanks for the life I have. I'm grateful each and every day. Nor do I need Mother's Day to tell my mother how much I love her or Valentine's Day to express to my wife the love, affection and appreciation I have for her. I don't need a holiday to brainwash me into behaving a certain way.

So Jack, that's nice, but where are you going with all this! My point is I can't believe what's happening to people in our towns, cities, states and throughout the country today. I can't believe the hatred, the violence, the distrust, the disunity that prevails everywhere I go. I can't believe that people actually have to guard their opinion here in America, in the land of the free and the home of the brave, where we are protected by our right to free speech.

I'm not a political person. Nor am I promoting one side over the other. Yes I have views and preferences, they have never been party specific and thus they are irrelevant to this discussion. What is relevant is people's attitudes and behavior regardless of which side they stand on.

Yet as people's behavior goes, no one is thinking oh what a great country we have become when a New York Giant's fan gets beat up in Philadelphia for wearing his Giants jersey in the parking lot around Veteran's Stadium where the Philadelphia Eagles play. It used to be you were allowed to have a preference, to like one team better. Yes there were heated arguments, great debates and shouting but at the end of the day there was not violence and hatred.

The Yankees Red Sox rivalry has been one of the greatest of all time. I remember in the early 70's being a 14 year old kid hanging around Yankee Stadium collecting autographs. As Yankee fans we hated the Red Sox, but that never stopped me from getting the autographs of Carl Yastrzemski, George Scott, Jim Lonborg, Rico Petrocelli, Tony Conigliaro, Carlton Fisk, Mike Andrews and a host of other Red Sox greats… And they signed autographs for us while we were wearing our Yankee hats! They knew we were the enemy! Why did they do it? They understood we were just picking sides and it wasn't personal. Everyone enjoyed the intensity of the game and the excitement of a good rivalry. I remember after the game the players would be dressed in a civilian clothes and head out of the stadium to the team bus to go to the hotel. And looking for more autographs we got to interact with the players… and see they were real people with real families doing real jobs… Oh yes they happen to be on the wrong team… and we conveniently and consistently told them so… and of course we yelled "you stink" from the stands… but face-to-face we thanked them graciously for taking time to stop and sign an autograph. They weren't required to do that, but they did it out of common decency and tolerance. Common decency and tolerance… What happened to that? I know times have changed and we are supposed to change with the times. We have the Internet and new technology that has wonderful benefits and blessings… But you know not every change is a good one. Somethings should stay the way they were, common decency and tolerance being the default behavior of people in America is one of those things that should've stayed the same… unfortunately it seems to me, it has not.

You see there were always boundaries! And everyone knew what the boundaries were. When the game started we rooted and cheered for our team. When it ended, the game was over. Now I understand that the future of our country and the laws of the land are not a game or sporting event. Indeed they will affect and impact the country and our future for generations to come. Yet I have seen intense fights in courtrooms, I have seen corporations and people going at each other like tigers in a cage, but always with boundaries, always within the rules of the court or the game… and it's always with the hope that truth and justice will prevail. Yet sometimes it was he who was a better tactician, a better planner, he who could find loopholes to make justice work in his favor, or he who had more financial resources who won.

But nevertheless they still did it within the boundaries of the game.

Now it breaks my heart today to see American against American, family member against family member, neighbor against neighbor, state against state as if this was Armageddon… It's not! And you know what the next political party will have the chance in two years to change things and somewhere along the line the balance of power will shift again… as it always does! And of course they will reverse what the other guy did and restore the world to the way they think it should be…And when one parties in power the other party is never happy and vice versa. Just as Yankee fans were never happy when the Red Sox were winning championships and vice versa…That my friends is just part of the game of life… And that is the way it played.

But we have a choice! We can choose to love or choose to hate! And you don't get to blame your choice or actions on some holiday like New Year's Eve or St. Patrick's Day. With no disrespect intended to my Irish friends, I am just pointing to the holiday as an example of people's behavior gone wild. At its core, it is a wonderful celebration of a great man who became recognized as a saint. I'm writing this holiday season to call timeout and remind us God gives us an example to love others and tells us to do that. Jesus tells us we are to pray for those who hurt us and we are to love our enemies as well as those that love us. It is an ideal based on the life of Jesus himself, that we are to love others unconditionally, regardless of how they behave and in doing so we are glorifying Jesus who lived a sacrificial life showering the world with unconditional love. Whether you agree with my view and belief in God or not, whether you agree with Christianity and Jesus Christ or not, you can still agree with the concept of something being a good idea.

I am not a Buddhist but I believe in many of the ways the Buddha says people should be treated, because they're good ideas. They represent good ways to treat people. You don't have to be a Christian or believe in a particular spiritual concept to have an innate sense of common decency or respect for others and the good judgment to understand that we need to share the planet (and the street we live on) in order to survive. So as Americans how did it get to be that we can no longer tolerate each other's opinion? How is it possible that I have to worry about letting my high school kid wear a hat that expresses his views because I fear someone may not like it and beat the crap out of him, for liking one team, person or ideal instead of the other.

I really don't care who is president. I care that the president cares about the people in this country and moves and acts in their best interest. I have loved some Democratic presidents and some Republican presidents and disliked some of each party and I find myself feeling the same way about candidates in other offices... it is usually not about the party but about the person and what they represent and stand for that matters to me, but that's a whole separate issue. The issue is about you and me in America and why we shouldn't tolerate the lack of common decency from people. No sooner than we would tolerate people parading naked around our little kids. No sooner than we tolerate people handing out free heroin or crack cocaine to our teenagers. Why wouldn't we tolerate that... because it's unacceptable! It's wrong! And we're not going to allow that to happen. And that should be our same attitude about how we behave towards each other. We should behave civilly and in love.

We should be allowed to disagree and you should be allowed to wear the hat and shirt you want to wear, wherever you want to wear it. And guess what? We all know everybody's got a hat and a shirt. Everybody's got a team and a candidate. Everybody's got a favorite band, a favorite song and a favorite movie. Everybody's got a favorite food. We get it! We all have opinions and preferences and in this great country were allowed to express them and say this is what I like, whether it's regarding God, sexuality, food, geographic location, education, politics and a host of other topics. This is America. This is why people want to be here. This is what is so great about our country.

It breaks my heart that we ourselves are the ones ruining it. Oh God that it would never be said of you and I that we were not peace makers. That we took to putting on a mask and using the insanity covering of the world to behave like idiots in an ungodly manner, rather I pray that we would turn towards God. That we would share the love of God with our neighbors. That we be tolerant and accepting of each other's views, thoughts, ideas and theories on life. We don't have to like people ideas but we are called to love people. It's easy to make exceptions for family members and close friends that we love and overlook things as it relates to them. Why? Because we love them. They belong to us. Yet we need to do it more for those we don't love and respect!

2018

I have been a Bruce Springsteen's fan since I'm 17 years old. I love Bruce Springsteen's music and anybody who knows me knows that. But I have never been a big fan of Bruce's politics, but you know what it never bothered me when Bruce talk politics during his concerts. It bored me after a while but it never bothered me that Bruce was using his platform to express his views... good for him. He earned that platform and the right to use it as he saw fit and speak from his heart. I didn't have to buy a ticket to see his show. Nobody forced me to listen. I love the music and it was well worth it and I love Bruce regardless of his political views. I think he is a wonderful person, a great individual, I think he has cared for and shared and given more to his fans then any public performer in the history of rock 'n roll... that's what makes him a unique and special person whose transparency and caring is heartfelt. So, it's up to you and I to take a stand against the poisoning division that is gripping our country todayz

When people asked me to define myself as a person, I answer I'm a Christian... I don't answer I'm of any particular denomination. Yet regardless of our beliefs about God we would all say we are Americans! I'm an American first... not a Floridian, not a New Yorker, but an American. I love America and its people. My point is we may have different opinions and thoughts but we share the land. Maybe it's time to go back and listen to that great folk classic by Woody Guthrie "This Land Is Your Land" and on a separate note if you want some personal inspiration for your life, go back and listen to Robert Goulet singing "To Dream The Impossible Dream" that will fire you up and motivate you.

As for me, I don't drink (or drive) on New Year's Eve. I don't drink or go out on St. Patrick's Day. I don't put on a costume on Halloween and throw eggs at people houses and I don't go nuts on the 4th of July. I'm not saying there is anything wrong with those things, but what I am saying is I don't need a particular excuse to do those things. If I want to set off fireworks I will. 365 days a year or any day I want. If I want to get rip-roaringly drunk and scream. I will. 365 days a year or any day I want. If I want to drink green beer I will 365 days a year or any day I want. I don't need an excuse to do it and you shouldn't need an excuse to be who you are. So OK this section of our letter is a little serious... but I hope it will rally you into not just standing on the sidelines and letting this happen and read about it. I hope you will make the statement that is not okay to hate each other and beat each other up for differences of opinions. There was intense racial separation in this country for a long time and it probably still exists unfortunately to some degree today. But I think a lot of racial healing has taken place and we know we are all brothers.

We are one person... each a part of the team, each with an important role to play. We get the concept in sports. We get each player does his part for the team and they're all part of the team and they win the championship together. We need to get that aspect in life. We are all individuals, with a calling and a job and a purpose and we do that the best we can. One of those purposes is to love each other and be kind to each other and show love and acceptance. It doesn't mean we have to agree, it doesn't mean we have to like each other's thoughts or opinions and it doesn't mean that we have to listen to everything everyone says. But it does mean that we have to tolerate others as we want them to tolerate what we say and do. I believe the word of God says it best when Jesus says "do onto others as you would have them do unto you". Personally I would like people to be able to wear any shirt or hat they want without getting the crap beat out of them, without getting yelled at, without getting their food spit in at a restaurant because somebody disagrees with their view. (I am adding a disclaimer ...none of this tolerance applies to criminals and mad men who are out to hurt you or kill you because they're insane, crazy or just stupid idiots. I would think that goes without saying).

I love the media. I love television. I've always loved platforms to be able to express ourselves, whether it's theater, movies, TV, radio, advertising, print and now the internet... anything! But I was taught long ago by some people that I admire very much that I always need to make sure I know the truth for myself. That teaching came from my mother and father, my brother, Bob Dylan, my ninth grade English teacher Patricia Dichiaro and my 11th grade high school English teacher Bill Blanchard who all taught me that I am responsible for my own decisions and my own thoughts and actions. That the words I hear from people, regardless of the platform they used to deliver them, including a pulpit I might add, are not always the truth! But I am responsible for knowing the truth and I have the ability and right to decide what I believe is true. Of course it's a good idea in your life and in my life if the truth is based on facts... Sometimes there are no facts to substantiate our belief of truth... that's okay too... but where there are facts we should definitely take them into account! So this holiday season I ask you to take a look at what the truth is... what is inside of you ...what you believe God wants you to do... what you want to do... and that you would act accordingly.

We know the media is slanted. We understand that. So that comes as no surprise. I understand when the Democrats speak he's going to talk about his views, and when the Republican speaks he's going to talk about the views of his party. I understand that when I go to a rock 'n roll concert I'm going to hear rock 'n roll, and when I go to the opera I'm going to hear opera and when I go to hear a country music concert I'm going to hear country music. I understand that people speak in the platform they want to speak in... that is not a secret to me. Yes I may have a preference of one style of music, genre of movie or political view verse the other... but it doesn't mean the other should be abolished and only my type of music should be allowed. It doesn't mean the other teams should go away and only my team should play. No that's not the country that we live in... or at least it didn't used to be.

So I hope and pray this holiday season you will deliberately go about being great. That you will sit down with someone you oppose politically and go out of your way to make it a point to let them know that regardless of our differing opinions of politics... or anything else for that matter... that you respect them as people... that you love them and that you believe that peace should rule our great country and believe we should treat each other with dignity and respect...and that you would live and act accordingly.

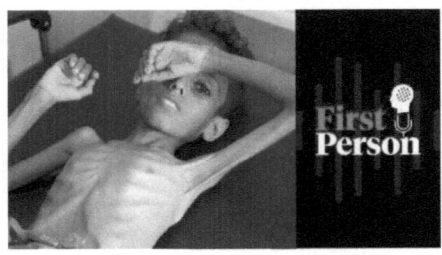

REMEMBER TO CARE!

I was reading the New York Post the other day and saw a picture that broke my heart. Now you and I have seen pictures like this before of starving children I don't know why this one particularly bothered me so much, but for me it represented all of the starving children, all of the suffering children in the world! This boy's name is Ghazi Ali bin Ali and I am praying for him. It is doubtful I'll be able to change his life as he is in Yemen, but it is a reminder that you and I have so much, so much, and yet we focus on what we don't have, instead of being grateful for what we do. I hope this holiday season you go out of your way to remember those that are suffering and to make a difference anywhere you can whether it's financially, spiritually, emotionally, relationally or physically... any way that you can. It does matter! We may not be able to save everyone, but if you can save one, you are way ahead of the game... it's the "starfish" story... you know it well (if not google it) ...now it's time to put it into practice.

BRING ON 2019 BABY!!!

Looking forward to 2019. Thank you Lord for my wonderful family who are such a blessing to me. We pray blessings to all of you this holiday season... for you and your families... that you would be at peace with yourselves, at peace with others, and most importantly that you would be at peace with God and that your relationship with God would grow intimately and excitingly. I pray you continue to take God up on His promise that if we come closer to Him, He will come closer to us (James 4:8).

Hard to believe my father has been physically gone from us for over a year. I am finding myself listening to a lot more Dixieland jazz (Dad's favorite music) these days it's like Dad is sitting in the car with me when I'm listening. I can still see him smile and talking about Dixieland music. The bottom line is he's not gone...he is as alive today in my heart as he has ever been. I consider that a remarkable present and gift from God. So you should take that to heart... your life does matter! The things you do and the people you impact do matter and will be remembered long after you're gone! So I repeat as my awesome cousin the great Robbie Grossman said so eloquently... "we'll all be in a grave at some point...let's make the time we have count!

God bless you guys we love you all the best from sunny FLA.

Jack, Beth, Jackson and Talia

December 2019

FAMILY UPDATE

Hello Most Awesome Family and Friends,

Happy Holidays! Merry Christmas! I hope you're excited about 2019. We pray it was a great year for everybody and hope that you are looking forward to 2020 with excitement, enthusiasm, and expectation!

REFLECTIONS ON LIFE!
CLICHES THAT ARE NOT TRUE

On the subject of clichés that are not true, how about the one that says, "there are two sides to every story, but the truth usually lies in the middle." No; that's a crock… Not the point of the two sides to every story, but the part about the truth "always" lying in the middle. Sometimes the truth is directly on one side or on the other and sometimes in the middle, but not always. That's a good reminder that things are not always what they seem or what other people say they are. Well, I could quit right here as that is pretty insightful, but what the heck since it's holiday time I'll give you a little more. So, here are a few bottom-line points that I hope will encourage and inspire you this year.

2019

THE RIGHT ATTITUDE

My buddy Charlie is 80 years old; Charlie and I both attend a weekly Tuesday morning bible study. He's a wonderful man of God and a wonderful human being. He was leaving to go on a mission trip, to Louisiana, and I said, "Charlie, that's so great. I'm so impressed and inspired that you would go out and do that. Without missing a beat he said, "You can't do too much to help people." Charlie has inspired me with the humbleness, actions, and faith of his life. And he never ceases to amaze me. He truly lives his life sold out for God and embodies many of the characteristics of Jesus in human form. Charlie's an inspiration and a blessing to me. I pray that the same would be said of you and me. Remember it's not what you say that counts, it's how you live and what you do!

YOU THINK YOU GOT TROUBLES?

Former NFL defensive tackle and three-time Pro bowl player, Tommy Harris, gave this amazing testimony about handling unimaginable tragedy, trial, and tribulation in his life. I pray it inspires you. Remember to focus on

God and His sovereignty and love for you! Harris opened up about the unimaginable tragedies that upended his life and reinforced his faith in God.

"I look at a miracle every day when I look in the mirror and see that I'm not in a straitjacket or have lost my mind for what I've been through," he said. "I'm a walking testimony. God moves every day through me, encourages me, inspires me to help someone else beyond myself."

"My wife was going in to have a breast reduction surgery. We were married for 41 days," Harris recalled. "I was on a plane... never knowing that when we land, I would get a phone call that said my wife stopped breathing on the table and I needed to hurry up and get to Oklahoma. I end up flying to Oklahoma. My wife was dead when I got there," Harris said he watched his new bride languish on life support for three days before he made the decision to let her go.

"I had to pull the cord on my wife at 28 years old, having millions of dollars, and nothing could help me at that moment. I lost all purpose for finances, for everything," he said. "That was the biggest time I believe my faith was tested, and I remember pulling the cord and I told

God to let His will be done in my life." The death of Harris' wife would not be the last tragic misfortune to test him. "I waited four years later to get back into a relationship with another woman, we end up having a kid. And four months later, we walked in the room and our daughter had passed away of SIDS, Sudden Infant Death Syndrome. I believe that God is speaking to me to show people how valuable life is and at any moment the game can change," he said. "So, are you playing your hardest at every moment?"

"I think that my breath right now is being used to teach that suddenly... things can change. And with the faith in God, you know that He'll never put more than you can bear." Harris also said his experiences and faith have encouraged him to do more and reach out to others in need. "I remember walking in the airport after I lost my wife, and I was about 300 pounds and I was just crying, walking through the airport," Harris recalled. "And I wanted someone to hold me, hug me or to notice me. But I realized at that moment that everyone was on their own schedules and nothing stops for anyone. So now, because of what I've been through, when I go to the airport, my head is on a swivel. I'm looking for the slumped-over shoulders. I'm looking for the guy that may not look approachable, but I know he needs a hug. So, I've learned from that situation to take it and help serve someone else."

GOD IS REAL

For whatever it's worth, I hope and pray you come to the point where you know God is real. I was asking myself this question the other day. "How much does my father love me?" I thought of how much my own father loved me. (It's been two years since he passed away.) I was the recipient of the greatest father ever; his love for me was unconditional, sacrificial, amazing, and continuous. What a blessing. I feel the same about my children although I don't know that I demonstrate it to them as well as my dad and mom did to me. But the point is God is real. His love for us is real. I pray this is a great treasure and comfort in your life!

THE MEANING OF DREAMS

If you're a regular reader of my holiday letters, perhaps you remember one year I slipped in the fact that I believe drinking hot chocolate or eating chocolate ice cream or

Oreo cookies before bedtime enhances my dreams. I call it the "Chocolate Factor". I've known this for many years and I have shared it with a few close friends and family. Recently a study came out that confirmed that chocolate has a psychoactive effect on the mind. No surprise to me! I have enjoyed my dreams over the years as they have been enhanced and made quite spectacular. I believe because of the chocolate. But I started to think about what the dreams really meant and how much I've enjoyed getting to the underlying meaning of so many of them. I thought I'd share this with you. This is my perception, my belief, and my definition of what dreams are and how they work. By the way, be sure to test out my "Chocolate Factor Theory" for yourself before bedtime one night!

So What Are Dreams and How Do they Work? Here's my theory. A particular random word or thought from the day gets a priority assignment in the subconscious mind. The mind keys in on that thought or word, then in a random shuffle of some subconscious deck, starts dealing them out as dreams, with the dream story being created around that random keyword or thought that the subconscious mind grabbed a hold of during the day. However, all these new dreams are keyed to specific underlying issues you are thinking about, real life stuff you are dealing with, for example; fear, stress, worry, etc. Yet these dream created stories are unrelated to the random thought of the day that was first processed into a dream. For example, I was watching the movie "The Jerk" one day and one character said something about Syracuse. It was an obscure, irrelevant line in the movie, but that night I had a dream about being back in college at Syracuse University. I woke up in the morning and could not figure out for the life of me why I had suddenly dreamed about Syracuse out of the blue, after so many years. But then I remembered the obscure line from the movie that day, and realized that's where I heard it.

So, even though you are dreaming dreams that the subconscious mind processed out to you and created for you based on a random word or thought picked up during the day, all of the dreams lead back and are tied to your subconscious's underlying fears, thoughts, worries, and concerns. So, that if you examine and interpret the dreams in terms of what you are struggling with; fears, thoughts, concerns, worries, etc., you will see how they tie into your life and what they really mean. So the feelings and emotions of the dream you experience are real, the story and settings are not.

The underlying factor that makes us dream, the underlying purpose of our dreams, is to see what is really lying behind and in the subconscious mind. It is the subconscious, which is held prisoner by the conscious, trying to break out into the conscious and in effect getting its moment in the sun, to shine and tell IT'S STORY. In essence, it is your subconscious knocking on your conscious trying to tell you to "wake up" and see what the issues really are! I know this is heavy and deep, but I think as it's Christmas I might as will give you everything I have. Smile! Plus, you guys are my friends, so now you can't ever say I was holding out you!

THE VALUE OF FAMILY HARMONY

We went to my nephew Zachary's wedding in October. It was unbelievable and awesome… so great to have family and friends together. The best part of it was it was a three day event. We flew in on a Friday somewhere in the middle of nowhere in Connecticut and all of the family and wedding party and friends stayed at a hotel. So, we had a rehearsal dinner and party Friday night, then we had the after dinner party Friday night, breakfast

Saturday, the wedding Saturday afternoon, after the wedding party Saturday night, then breakfast Sunday morning. It was just everybody together for three days of fun, fellowship, family and love. It was wonderful. It was so heartwarming and special, it made me realize that this must be the dream of every father and mother to see their family together and happy. I am certain that is God's will for us as well when He tells us to live in unity with each other, love each other, that we are all part of the same family. But this was an earthly glimpse of what heaven must be like as it was a total sharing of love, joy, happiness, hope, laughter. All ages coming together for a single purpose… to celebrate. It was awesome! I hope this holiday you get to celebrate and experience something similar with those you love.

MY FRIEND GEORGE GOES TO AFRICA

My friend and wonderful, spiritual mentor here in Orlando, Pastor George Cope, teaches an incredible bible study on Tuesday mornings. I've been going for years. In early October, George was going on a mission trip to the Congo for a few weeks to train pastors. Before he left he was teaching our Tuesday morning bible study class. After the bible study, I was driving home and I was so overwhelmed by the spirit of God speaking to my heart regarding George and his trip that I pulled over to send him a text. Here's what it said…

"George, great to see you this morning brother. I will be continuing to pray for your trip Monday. I know God will bless it. I'm praying that you stay well as I know you want to be at full strength to deliver God's message. As I was driving home today, I had a clear vision of a pastor walking up to you and saying these exact words, "I never would believe that God could speak to me in such a way." I am praying you not only hear this, but many other messages of affirmation and gratitude for being God's messenger to those wonderful pastors. Love you brother. To God be the glory, Jack"

He texted back that afternoon: "Thanks Jack. I'm really excited to meet the person who will say to me, 'I never could believe God could speak to me that way.'"

On October 14, the day before he was coming home from Africa, he texted, "Morning Jack! Just wanted you to know I met the man that spoke your prophetic words. It happened Friday in an unanticipated speaking opportunity. I walked into a room full of pastors and they asked me to speak. That night, I spoke in one of these pastor's churches and he told me exact words you said would happen! God is so faithful. Love you brother. George"

Now, I don't claim to be a prophet by nature, but I've had certain instances my life when God has spoken so clearly and directly, there is no doubt it is the Spirit of God speaking. I always enjoy when I have the privilege of seeing God's Word in action and His power at work in this earthly life. There is no doubt in my mind that all of God's promises and words are true, and will be true for all eternity. I will get to see all of them fulfilled. Of course, with God's Holy Spirit residing in my heart, I always have access to God. And don't forget, as a believer in Christ, you have the same access! Thank you, Jesus, for paying the price, so I would have individual and first-hand access to God on this earth and for all eternity. The great news for all of you this holiday season is God's gift is available to all!

2019

JACKSON'S ARGUMENT AND PREMISE

My son Jackson could be a genius... Or at least an excellent lawyer! Unfortunately for me, my kids Jackson and Talia have long ago learned the art of winning at negotiation. Hopefully, it will pay for my retirement. Right now, I'm just getting the snot beat out of me. Smile! Anyway, I hope you'll see the beauty of this point Jackson raised to me the other day.

Jackson mentioned to me that he wanted to go somewhere. I said, "Son, you can't go there because you need to be 21 to get into that place." Without missing a beat, he responded, "but I identify as 21." I laughed. Jackson lost the battle and didn't get to go... because he's not 21! However, I can't wait to hear his next argument and premise... smile! Just as when he turned 16 and got bigger he was finally able to beat me in basketball, I believe the day is coming when he will out argue me, out logic me and win in that arena too, right now I'm just grateful to still be in the game... and I'm trying to kick his butt (and win the arguments and negotiations) as much as possible while I still can!

PERSPECTIVE

A young friend of mine who is just 15 was going through some issues with drug use and addiction. As I sat and talked with him, I realized he was sharing with me his perspective, which was that of a 15-year-old. I have great respect for him and acknowledge his perspective, but I realized there was so much he had not seen and so much he did not know because of experiences he had not yet had, roads he had not yet traveled down and places he had not yet gone… But I had traveled down those roads, been there and seen them, and could tell him exactly where those roads lead.

God spoke to my heart and reminded me this is what heaven is like. God says, "Now you know in part, then you'll know in full." (lst Corinthians 13:12) Here's what I mean… How easy would it be if my friend would just listen to my advice? How much better would his life be? How much pain and sorrow could he eliminate and not have to go through? But he is stubborn. He has his own perspective and I'm sure he'll make his own choices. Just like me. And just like you. I pray that I (and you) will trust God and not have to make so many mistakes and feel so much pain that is completely avoidable.

2019

THE STORY OF THE LAKE

It was in July of this year and we were at grandma Sally's house in Cazenovia, New York. I was sitting at Cazenovia Lake on the bandstand, I was able to see across the lake. On the other side of the lake were some very large trees. I know the road behind those trees leads to Manlius, then continues on to Fayetteville, then continues on to Syracuse. I know that because I have been driven down that road many times over the last 15 years. God shared with me that our lives are the same way. He loves us and is trying to tell us exactly where the road leads and how to go because He knows it. He created it. I believe that's a great parallel regarding Gods love for us and the path to heaven and eternal salvation. I pray you will take it to heart. AND YES, I KNOW I CAN'T SEE THE FUTURE, BUT I CAN SEE GOD AND HIS KINGDOM AND THAT'S ENOUGH FOR ME!

WHAT ARE YOU SCARED OF?

Either God is a liar or He's not… If He's not, you are an idiot to worry!

I was driving an older friend to the doctor one day. It was raining very, very hard on the way, brutally hard. It was hard to see even with the wipers going full speed. My friend was upset and praying as we drove, "Oh God please don't let anything happen to us." I was reassuring him I had everything under control. I had driven in situations like this many times going to college in Syracuse, living in New York, and in tremendous thunderstorms in South Florida over the years. While this was an inconvenient driving situation and not what I prefer, it was not life-threatening and I had it under control. The more I reassured him everything was under control, the more he worried and panicked, saying it was his fault for making me take him to the doctor and that he should never have come, which was pretty absurd since he needed to go and it was my pleasure to take him.

Eventually the rain subsided. The bottom line is he worried and panicked for nothing, just like the disciples in the boat when the waves began to crash around them, they panicked and thought Jesus had deserted them. Either my friend didn't believe me or didn't have enough faith in me to not panic. He got scared by his own fear and imagination of how the situation might end, with no faith in the assurance I was giving him, no faith in what the ending I assured him would be! No wonder non-believers are scared of dying! They have no faith in the assurance God has promised and not enough faith to believe in Him. I believe that is a tragedy.

We are to remember no matter what is happening in our lives, God's is saying to us, "I got this; I am in control." It reminded me of when I learned to drive harness horses, learned to play professional Jai-Alai, went rappelling down a 60-foot building, or was flying on a trapeze in circus school… Once you've learned it and done it well, you are not afraid. But in the beginning, it is terrifying!

WHAT REALLY MATTERS!

Here's a story that someone shared with me, author unknown, I believe it will speak to your heart about the value of life.

A billionaire, with a fortune of $7 billion, died at the age of 56 from pancreatic cancer. Here are some of his last words: "In other's eyes, my life is the essence of success, but aside from work, I have little joy, and in the end, wealth is just a fact of life to which I am accustomed. At this moment, lying on the bed, sick and remembering all my life, I realize that all the recognition and wealth I have is meaningless in the face of imminent death. You can hire someone to drive a car for you, make money for you — but you cannot rent someone to carry the disease for you. One can find material things, but there is one thing that cannot be found when it is lost — 'life.'

Treat yourself well and cherish others. As we get older, we are smarter and we slowly realize that whether that watch is worth $30 or $500 — both show the same time. Whether we carry a purse worth $20 or $300 — the amount of money in the wallets are the same. Whether we drive a car worth $15,000 or a car worth $300,000 — the road and distance are the same, we reach the same destination. If we drink a bottle worth $300 or wine worth $10 — the 'buzz' will be the same. If the house we live in is 600 square feet or 9000 square feet — the loneliness is the same. Your true inner happiness does not come from the material things of this world. Whether you're flying first class, or economy class — if the plane crashes, you crash with it. So, I hope you understand that when you have friends or someone to talk to — this is true happiness!"

So, Here's some good advice:

1. Do not educate your children to be rich. Educate them to be happy, so when they grow up, they will know the value of things, not the price.

2. Eat your food as medicine, otherwise you will need to eat your medicine as food.

3. Whoever loves you will never leave you, even if he has 100 reasons to give up. He will always find one reason to hold on.

4. If you want to go fast – go alone! But if you want to go far – go together!

GOD SPEAKS TO US PERSONALLY!!

I wanted to share this with you. It is a text I received from a friend of mine on July 13 of this year, his soon to be married 26-year-old son died in a tragic car crash last year! I pray it will impact you and speak to your heart and change your perspective dramatically as it did mine.

"My wife and I have a tough day ahead. Not that all days are not tough but today my son is gone one year. I still can't believe it. We are going out to the ocean buoy where we put his ashes with some close friends and going to remember my son. When tragedy strikes as this has stricken my wife, myself and my family it changes your whole life. The pain of losing my son always weighs on me. I work, I live, but I am not the same person. You don't get over this, you don't accept this, you survive this. A piece of me has died. I am very thankful for my grandson and my wife and my friends and family it could always be worse. When something like this tremendous tragedy happens to someone it is life altering and forces you to think about eternity and makes you want so bad to believe in God in Heaven and that I will one day see my son again and that life they call eternity will be all the bible says it will be, which is a blissful life of love and vividness and high sensitivity and no pain and no greed and no anger and no jealousy and on and on. Enjoy your weekend. Love your kids love your wife and family. Tomorrow is promised to no one".

MURRAY

I was at a family party this year with a family friend, MURRAY, who at 93 years old has more life, energy, hope, and joy in him them most 30 year olds I know. His first wife Fran died a few years ago and he shared this bottom line thought with me… "When we went through four years of suffering with Fran's cancer before her death, we found out what was important and what was not."

BE CLEAR ON THIS!!

You have the same amount of God available to you as I do!! Or anyone else! Like kids at a dinner table with their parents… All the kids have access to the parents! As God has already spoken directly to us, just listen to His Word and take it to heart. Like Bob Dylan, Bruce Springsteen or other great poets and songwriters, if you want to know what they were thinking, just listen to what they said in their songs or read what they wrote. Remember Matthew 4:4 says, "Man does not live by bread alone, but by every word that comes out of the mouth of God."

THE PARABLE OF GOD AND THE SPRINGSTEEN TICKET

So, let me wrap it up by explaining it to you like this. You know I'm a Springsteen fan and here's how I view God and the kingdom of heaven. It's like a Springsteen concert… You see, if Bruce was having a concert (and yes he's touring in 2020, hope to see you there!), and I already had my ticket, I would be telling you to go and get a ticket yourself because I know how great and amazing it will be and because I would want you to experience it for yourself. At the end of the day, while I sincerely hope you get your ticket and see the concert, I will be rejoicing and celebrating that I had mine, knowing for certain that no matter what, I was going to be there. That's how I view God's love, mercy, grace, promise of eternal salvation and Holy Spirit living inside of us. The greatest thing ever. And I want you to have it and share in it and not to miss it! Remember we know that most Bruce concerts seem like they are never ending because he plays for so long, sometimes up to four hours, but the truth of the matter is they do end… But God's love and eternity never does! So make sure you have your ticket!

ARE YOU HUNGRY?

Many Christians say they want more "meat" in their sermons and messages and that is a wonderful thought. However, knowing the color of the sand Moses walked on in the desert may be an interesting fact, but I would consider that a snack. The real "MEAT" is in what

JESUS SAID, (anything else is just a snack) and it's all the meat we'll ever need to be thoroughly fed for this life and the one to come in eternity! Don't forget to chew on it thoroughly and enjoy it!

LIFE INSPIRATION

Lastly, I want to leave you with some life inspiration and I pray something that will impact your heart and mind, and allow you to live in the freedom that God created you for.

It's Luke 1:73-74, God tells us he swore an oath to our father Abraham and that was "to rescue us from the hand of our enemies and to enable us to serve him without fear." It is a privilege and honor to live on this earth with whatever time God has allocated for us here and exciting to think that we get to spend all eternity with Him when our time on earth is up. But God has given us another privilege as well the ability to know Him and love Him and live for Him… and that is to live without fear all of our days! I pray you would not be fooled or distracted by Satan or the things of this world or with desires of the flesh, and miss out on the joy of the Lord. Remember God says "it is for freedom you have been set free by Christ"!

TIME GONE VOLUME 2

Live joyfully and live free! Merry Christmas, Happy Holidays and Happy New Year!

Love Jack, Beth, Jackson and Talia

December 2020

TIME GONE VOLUME 2

FAMILY UPDATE

Happy holidays to all our wonderful family and friends! People say this year went by really fast and in the spirit of this surprising, unexpected year I am going to see if we can do the same thing with this letter. So surprise… No long letter!

I could tell you how much we miss our families in Cazenovia and Scarsdale, New York as obviously we have not seen them for over a year now.

I could also tell you that in the insanity of this year that the silver lining from the Covid 19 virus for Beth and I was all the quality time we got to spend with Jackson and Talia in March and April. We hated the suffering and death that was brought about by Covid 19, but we did love the time with our kids. It was a time we will cherish and remember for the rest of our lives. Thank God the vaccine is coming for those who choose to take it, and hopefully 2021 will go down as the year Covid was no more, and you will be able to resume life as you knew it (although perhaps with fewer handshakes)!

2020

And I could recap this crazy year by saying we probably saw more action in our country this year than I can recall since the riotous, revolutionary days of the late 60s, as the passion and tension that tore across our country (whether you agreed with its reasons or not) this year were similar in intensity and violence (both real and perceived) to revolutionary actions of the 60's.

This year, the political tensions in a country divided caused tremors felt across every state. I pray people will unite regardless of political preferences and points of view! This country is not about politics, it is about people and their hearts. It always has been and I pray always will be! May hearts, people, and families unite. After all, no matter how many things people want to change or pretend didn't happen or rewrite history to accommodate and suit their own needs and views, America was created to be one nation, under God, indivisible with liberty and justice for all! And that has not changed! You can erase the words from the history books, you can rewrite them, but you cannot take them out of our hearts and minds. This is the true foundation of our country and who we are. We were made to live it accordingly and may God always be a part of our lives in this country's past, present, and future.

I could talk about the insanity of this year's stock market, a severe crash in March and April and an incredible rebound as of the writing of this letter. Hope you stayed in! And there's probably 20 more things I could fill you in on from this year's events in our life that would either make you smile or cry! But I'm not going to do any of that this year.

And I could tell you why I'm not writing the usual 20 page Christmas letter full of life insights but keeping it short this year. Instead, I'm just going to leave you with a short story of inspiration written by a friend of mine (it's the last page of this letter). I hope it inspires you and I hope you remember the 3 most important things I can tell you. Here they are:

1. God loves you. Have an individual, personal relationship with God who is your Father, Creator, and Savior.

2. Love Others. As life was never meant to be lived alone. It is always about connection with other people. About validation, about friendship, about acceptance, and about love for others. Life has never been about taking, it is always been about giving. That is the true joy. Man was never meant

to be alone, we were always meant to be connected to each other and that is not only the best way to live… I believe it is the only way to live… and the only way that you can call your existence living.

3. Forgive Yourself. Finally, as the wise Proverb says, "He who gets wisdom loves his own soul." Remember, God has forgiven your sins, so it is probably a good idea to forgive yourself, as well. As that was clearly God's intention when He forgave you. He did not want you to carry the burden of guilt, shame, and failure around so that you are overwhelmed by those emotions and cannot enjoy your life. But instead He wants you to carry the love of your forgiving Father around so you are free to live, laugh, love, and enjoy your time here on Earth, as your life is truly a gift from God. God, your heavenly Father, who only wants to bless you, who understands that you make mistakes and that you're not perfect, loves you not for what you do, but for who you are and for whose you are. You are His. He has provided for an abundant life for you here on Earth and eternal life for you in Heaven if you should choose to believe… If you have that, you have the greatest gift of all!

Love to you all. Blessings and enjoyment be yours this holiday season and the year to come.

Jack & Beth, Jackson and Talia

Here is the inspiring letter from my friend:

THE ARTIST AND THE AUDIENCE
by Kennan Burch

The Artist has given me a ticket to His concert of life; His all-consuming music touches every part of me.

Everything I see, hear, touch, taste, smell, and even comprehend are all part of the music of The Artist. May I never forget that I am the audience and not the artist, that I am the receiver and not the giver!

For at times I'm tempted to summon The Artist to recognize me for my song, And to woo others in the audience to hear me too, But I find the sound of my song drowns out the music of The Artist. It is only when I lay down my own instrument and focus towards the stage, that I begin to hear music loud and clear, -- Music so consistent I cannot imagine an Artist with such rhythm -- Music so beautiful I cannot imagine an Artist with such creativity -- Music so vast I cannot comprehend an Artist so big-- Music so complex I cannot imagine an Artist with such intelligence -- Music so intricate I cannot imagine an Artist with such attention to detail-- Music so diverse I cannot imagine an Artist with such diversity -- Music so vibrant I cannot imagine and Artist with such life -- Music so freely given I cannot imagine an Artist with such love.

May I never choose to ignore the music of The Artist, or attribute it to mere happenstance, for therein would lie my greatest offense. It is written that The Artist knit me together in my mother's womb, that He knows when I get up, and when I lie down, and that He counts the very number of hairs on my head. For an Artist so great, to invite me to His concert, and play His songs for me... I am honored, I am humbled, and His music is certainly worthy of my attention.

May I not perform good works out of duty, but may I enjoy the music so much that my natural response is the applause of good works. May my life not be known for the things that I have done But for the music I hear, the praise I express, and for encouraging others to listen to the music. In so doing The Artist will be honored, I'll enjoy the concert, and maybe you might find new meaning behind the music and join in the applause of The Artist.

But the ultimate experience lies not in simply enjoying the music and applauding The Artist, it is found when I lay down my life and become an instrument in the hands of The Artist and he begins to play music through me, that is where I find meaning, purpose, and a heart that comes fully alive. May we all enjoy the music, applaud The Artist and become instruments of His music to a world in desperate need of hearing it.

CHRISTMAS Blessings

"Blessed is the one who trusts in the Lord." Psalm 40:4

December, 2021

TIME GONE VOLUME 2

FAMILY UPDATE

Hello Dear Friends and Family,

So, a crazy year for everybody, as we continue to deal with the ramifications of Covid 19 and a currently "unstable" (for lack of a better word) political and economic climate. But all in all, regardless of your views and/or sides and opinions, my belief is it is definitely great to be alive to see it all. I am trusting God and am thankful to live in our great country that allows us to live these wonderful lives. Lives of privilege, lives of purpose, lives of passion, and we pray for you a life of joy, health, and happiness.

I'm going to keep my letter shorter this year. I just want to share with you a couple of observations from two friends of mine and one from me. My friend Melissa is an inspiration to me and has been since I've known her. She had an auto accident, over a decade ago, after a night of drinking as a high school senior that has kept her in a wheelchair, with most of her body paralyzed since that day. Yet her attitude and optimism about life, her trust and faith in God, and her desire to impact the lives of so many, helping them avoid making the same mistakes of drinking and driving, are an inspiration to me. She is a national speaker, using her own life as an example as to the ramifications of drinking and driving.

The second observation is from my college friend Bruce who is unfortunately suffering from ALS, a crippling, life shortening disease, known as Lou Gehrig's disease. Bruce shared his perspective in a Facebook post about a particular encounter he had and how it caused him to look at his life and reevaluate his perspective on life. I hope and pray it will cause you to do the same.

The last observation is from me. It is something I wrote in July after reading some of God's promises from His word that He makes to all of His children, reminding myself of how much God loves me.

I do believe these are the three best Christmas presents I can give you and I hope they inspire and bless you.

So, to our wonderful friends and family; blessings to you all. We truly love you, appreciate you, and are blessed to know you. We give thanks to God for our wonderful lives. For even though there are times of turmoil, trial, and tribulation, I wouldn't trade any of it for the joy of being alive, experiencing life, love, laughter, and this wonderful journey called "life." Knowing for certain that when my time is up, I will be going home to be with God forever for all eternity. It is just a great deal that gets better and better! Thank you God. Merry Christmas to you all. Happy New Year! We love you.

Jack, Beth, Jackson & Talia

****

From Melissa (March 2021)

"Yesterday I met a man that was supposed to be on flight #5481 leaving Charlotte on 1/8/2003. His original flight the night before was overbooked and they asked 6 passengers to please give up their seat. The compensation would be a free hotel stay and a round trip to your destination of choice.

At the time he was dating a girl that went to Florida State University and he was thinking a free chance to see his girl couldn't have come at a better time. But then he remembered classes were starting tomorrow and if you weren't there for the first day of attendance that was an automatic drop. Torn with a hard decision he decided at the last minute to not give up his seat. He made it back to his dorm that night.

The next day, all over the news, was the story of the flight he would have taken if he had given up his ticket and went to see his girlfriend. Approximately 35 seconds after taking off something went terribly wrong, the plane crashed and everybody on that flight lost their life.

Yesterday morning when I met him, (he was sitting in a DUI class I was speaking at), after getting caught boating under the influence. I saw the pain of him reliving those details all over his face as he shared something that has torn him apart since 2003.

The day he could have lost his life was over 18 years ago. And nothing has been the same since. I think we all have at least one day that stands out unlike any other. It's a car accident. It's a miscarriage. It's an eviction notice. It's the day you lose your mom. It's you telling someone you'll love them forever and 4 years later they want a divorce. It's everything falling apart at once.

But it's also another chance.

I can't tell you how that last minute decision has impacted the rest of his life. But this is what I know…when it comes to God, you'll never run out of second chances, but you will run out of time. For some reason you and I are still alive today. So I say work hard on yourself every day to not dwell on the past. And don't get so caught up in building your future that you forget to be here right now. Because this, right now, and all of its mess, might be all you have left."

From Bruce Living Your Best Life: 2020 ALS, Covid and The Yellow Parakeet:

In May of 2019 a neurologist looked me in the eye and said you have ALS. I didn't hear much after that. It was a beautiful early spring day in Maine and all I knew was I needed to get out of that small antiseptic office and into the warm sunlight and listen to the birds. While I had been sick for over eight months, lost 65lbs and undergone numerous and invasive testing, with no diagnosis, ALS was never in my mind. Everything changed from that moment on. The journey is emotional and frightening. I am fortunate to have a large group of family, friends and co-workers who have rallied around me. An ALS support worker told me; "no day will be like the next," and she was so right.

I had to leave an executive corporate job and co-workers/friends that I enjoyed and who inspired me. I was always an extreme extrovert who ran on the energy of other people. I thrived on the ability to manage multiple projects, people, budgets – like the man spinning plates. The change to being retired at 62, ill and isolated was a shock that had me starting to question everything. My support group really helped me manage the daily ups and downs of emotions through my first year. I was having numerous lunches, coffees and happy hours with friends. My co-workers used to organize a monthly happy hour where 10 – 20 people would show up at a brew pub. I was able to walk and get around and was still active as a board member of the food bank here in Maine. As a Christmas present in 2019 I surprised my wife with a Caribbean cruise for the end of February. We also learned that night that our first grandchild would be born in May.

We boarded the ship on 2/23/20 and came home on 3/1/20. While on board I remember hearing Italy was shutting down their schools and thinking this Covid thing could be serious. In a flash Covid descended and like millions of others I was secluded in our house. We are so fortunate to have a nice home, be financially secure and live in a beautiful part of the country away from the "big" city. But the isolation began to weigh heavily on my psyche. Zoom is all well and fine but it does not replace real interaction. My 95-year-old mother passed away on

May 19 alone in her nursing home. 36 hours later our first grandchild Lilly was born. Both life altering events that had to be experienced from a distance. Through the summer, as my physical abilities continued to deteriorate, a friend with ALS said it's as if a thief comes every night and steals a little more of you. We purchased a single floor, handicap accessible condo and started the stressful process of moving and selling a home we lived in for 35 years.

During this entire time one of the ALS support groups I attended focused on mindfulness and meditation. During my business career and being a parent I began to understand the power of being in the present, living in the moment. To cope with ALS, this becomes essential as there is no cure. My life will end sooner than I ever imagined. I will not get to see Lily grow up, see my children flourish as adults, enjoy the golden years with my wife.

We had bird feeders in our yard for years and it became a popular spot for numerous birds all year round. There is a serenity to watching different birds come and go that I enjoyed even more as I was confined by both ALS and Covid. One day in September a bright yellow bird showed up among the brown and gray native birds of Maine.

We were informed he was a parakeet, but no one knew where he came from. Did he escape or did someone let him go? He would come to our yard every day to feed and bask in the sun. It became a source of joy and comfort to see him. We decided it was a "him" for no good reason.

A local woman with an avian connection began to try and capture him. Along with neighbors and others they would trudge through our field with nets. She spent months coming early mornings attempting to catch him. He was very fast and never allowed his pursuers to get close enough to capture him. We were told he could not take a Maine winter and needed to be caught if he was to survive. This sparked the discussion, was it better to catch him and put him back in a cage or let him live his new life, free, one day at a time. We moved into October and November, we started texting every morning when we would see him. There were some cold nights but he managed to survive. December came and he was still with us. On December 6, we had a snow storm. We were sure that was the end. But there he was the next morning, his beautiful yellow standing out against the snow. (See photo) The nights of December 7 & 8 were bitterly cold, and every morning I was so happy to see that patch of yellow among the brown branches in our yard. On the morning of 12/8 he landed on a lilac branch right in front of our window and we marveled at his beauty and resilience.

This was the last time we saw him. I still look out every morning hoping, but also content that he lived his best life on his terms, one day at a time. A philosopher once said: "If you are depressed you are living in the past. If you are anxious you are living in the future. If you are at peace you are living in the present."

****

From Jack (July 2021) I wrote this after reading some of God's awesome promises to His children in His word: "I have seen your glory here on earth Lord. I have experienced your miracles, mercy, and glory first hand. You amaze me Lord. I have been blessed with relationship with your Holy Spirit Lord. I am in awe of your power, majesty, grace, love, providence, and protection over my life. I can't even imagine the heaven/or heavenly kingdom and how awesome it will be, but I know Lord you have prepared a place for me in it. And I rejoice in your love for me, your protection and your provision. I am so blessed to be your child, to have experienced the kingdom here on earth. Your Holy Spirit inside of me. I watch in awe at the miracles you do and the providence and provision of your guiding hand on my life! Thank you, Father, for your joy and your peace – they are priceless – of more worth than any earthly pleasure, pursuit or item. I am filled with excitement Father to see what you have in store for me here on earth – how I may build your kingdom in my short time here – may I focus on what is important and not be distracted by the shiny, worthless items of the world but focus on the true treasure of the kingdom. I pray these things in the wonderful, mighty and precious name of Jesus – my awesome Lord, Savior and King! To God be the glory! In Jesus name I pray amen!"

2022

December 2022

TIME GONE VOLUME 2

FAMILY UPDATE

Dear Family and Friends,

Greetings from sunny Florida... definitely the greatest place on earth. It has been for me and my family as we have enjoyed the Florida sun, lifestyle, people, and community since 1985 (Beth 1998), and continue to be blessed living here.

We wish all of you a wonderful Happy Holiday, Merry Christmas, Happy Hanukkah, and the happiest of New Year's.

As I reflect back, I cannot believe that on March 10, 1991 I came to know Jesus as my personal Lord and Savior, and have had that blessing and benefit for almost half my life... thank you God. It just keeps getting better and better. I love God so much and He is not a liar when he says in Jeremiah 33:3, "Call on me and I will show you great and mighty things you did not know."

Just a few short thoughts to close out this year:

MOTIVATION AND INSPIRATION

I love this story and want to share with you if you're not familiar with it because it gives us a great perspective of life. I hope it is a tremendous blessing to you this holiday season and one you will think about cherish and will literally change your perspective on life

JUST IMAGINE YOU ARE INCREDIBLY RICH

Imagine that you have won the following PRIZE in a contest:

Each morning your bank deposits $86,400 in your private account for your personal use. However, this prize has specific rules:

1. Each morning, the bank deposits into your account $86,400 for that day.

2. You may not simply transfer money into some other account.

3. You may only spend it.

4. Everything that you didn't spend during each day would be taken away from you.

5. The bank can end the game without warning; at any time, it can say, "Game Over!"

6. It can close the account, and you will not receive a new one.

What would you personally do? Maybe you would buy anything and everything you wanted; not only for yourself, but for all the people you love and care for; maybe, even for people you don't know, because you couldn't possibly spend it all on yourself. No doubt, you would try to spend every penny and use it all, because you know it will be replenished the next morning, right?

ACTUALLY, THIS GAME IS REAL!

Each of us is already a winner of this PRIZE. We just don't realize it or think about it.

THE PRIZE IS "TIME."

1. Each morning each of us awakens to receive 86,400 seconds as a gift of life.

2. When we go to sleep at night, any remaining time is not credited to us.

3. What we haven't used up that day is forever lost.

4. Yesterday is forever gone.

5. Each morning the account is refilled, but your account can be dissolved at any time and WITHOUT WARNING.

So, what will YOU do with your daily gift of 86,400 seconds? Those seconds are worth so much more than the same amount in dollars.

Think about it and remember to enjoy every second of your life, because time races by so much more quickly than you think it will. Take care of yourself; love the Lord with all your heart, be happy, love deeply, and enjoy every second of the life you have been given! AND, START SPENDING!!

AUDIENCE OF ONE:

A good friend and retired pastor reminded me that he is living his life for an audience of one. That everything he does and says is done to hear the applause of God. God is his audience and if he can hear the applause of God he believes his life will have been well lived and well worth it. This is a joyful journey he is on and a great goal and foundational point for all of us to mirror and live by. After I heard it, I was inspired to do the same and matching and measuring my actions up against only one criteria… which is will God be pleased with this thought, action, or word I speak and what I do next. If I do that I can well expect my life would matter for the kingdom of God. Also that it would be filled with the joy, peace and happiness of the Lord as the things I am doing I am doing for Him. It is not the applause of others that matters or the reviews of critics or the cheers of the crowd or likes on social media… The only thing that matters is the applause of one… Your Lord God King and Savior… May you hear that applause every day of your life and for all eternity!

HARD TO SAY GOODBYE: Gone But Not Forgotten:

UNCLE SY: On a sad note, my Uncle Sy passed away in November at 98 years old. On a happy note, he lived to be 98 years old and was a wonderful loving man with a great family who loved him dearly. As a kid growing up, I spent many Sundays at Uncle Sy and Aunt Micky's house. Uncle Sy was a great guy. He was always happy. He showered us with love and encouragement and always put a smile and word of encouragement into every conversation. It is not a surprise to me that he lived so long as he was always able to see the sunny side of life. Even though he went through some difficult times in his own life, he never let the stress of circumstance or the problems of life destroy his spirit and love for life and people. Instead, he rose above it to spread joy and love to his family and friends. We are so blessed to be a part of his life and such a close-knit family for so many years and still to this day. God must really love me to have given me such a great family. Do not take for granted your family and those that love you… Not everybody is so fortunate.

2022

COUSIN GARY: Well, my awesome, one of a kind, amazingly kind-hearted and loving wonderful cousin Gary also died this year. Gary was born with Down Syndrome and they didn't expect him to live too long as a child... But he sure fooled them. He lived into his sixties! He spread love and joy everywhere to everyone he met. The tributes at his funeral poured in from staff, friends, and the other patient's families - the many many lives he impacted with his selfless, beautiful, child-like, and God-like love for all.

He touched my heart in such a big way. His innocence and love for people and life was so pure and true and unpolluted. It brought great joy to my heart to talk with him, to laugh with him, to hug him, to share ice cream with him, and just to see how happy and satisfied he is simply being alive. No panic about the past, no concern for the future, merely living in the joy of the moment and responding to each second and event as it occurs. I couldn't help but think back to the Bible passage in Matthew 18:3 where Jesus says we are to accept the kingdom of heaven like little children, with the complete belief and faith of a child, taking to heart every word their father says. Gary does just that.

When Gary hugged me, I could feel it in every inch of my body, every particle of my being. I felt as if I was hugging Jesus himself, as Gary's love overflowed and overcame me in the most wonderful way - a sweet reminder of the purity, fullness, and completeness of God's love.

I pray that you and I would align our hearts with God and enjoy the simple joys and pleasures God has given us in our lives. We should live in an attitude of gratefulness and appreciation and excitement for what today brings, enjoying each moment and not burdened by the passing of time, not wearied by unmet expectations, and not crushed by fear of the future… Just alive, being, living, loving, laughing… So, thank you, Gary, my wonderful cousin and God's child, for sharing your love so freely and for reminding me what really matters!

Unfortunately, my college buddy Bruce Daman passed away this year after suffering his last years of life with ALS, aka Lou Gehrig's disease, which is a crippling, life shortening disease. Bruce shared in a Facebook post last year, "In May of 2019 a neurologist looked me in the eye and said you have ALS. While I had been sick for over eight months, lost 65 lbs. and undergone numerous and invasive testing, with no diagnosis, ALS was never in my mind. Everything changed from that moment on. The journey is emotional and frightening. My life will end sooner than I ever imagined. I will not get to see my new granddaughter Lily grow up, see my children flourish as adults, or enjoy the golden years with my wife."

If you are reading this, YOU are still alive. We were born for fellowship, relationship, and connection. That is why God gave us hearts to love. Please do not take for granted the everyday joys and beauties of life; they are precious and it starts with people! If Bruce were still here, he would remind you how blessed you are to have them.

EVAN'S DAD: Here in Winter Garden a 23-year-old local man, Evan Fitzgibbons, who was serving in Georgia as an Army Ranger died this year in a tragic Army training accident. I did not know Evan or his family personally, but as part of a men's ministry group went out to his high school football field where they were holding a memorial for his life just days after he died. I was amazed that night as our community assembled at 7 PM to hear from Evan's high school principal, his football coach, and his pastor all share about his wonderful character and his commitment and love for God. But the moment that really shook me was when his mother and father took the stage to speak. His mother wearing sunglasses to hide her tears, simply thanked the crowd for coming and told her how much the community meant to her and Evan's family. Then his father John got up to the microphone and said these amazing words, "I thank God for the 23 years I had with Evan. I know, I know, I know where my son is now." That is the certainty of faith in Jesus Christ, of salvation and of our place in eternity. John Fitzgibbons did not get mad at God. He did not curse God. He did not say God didn't care about him. Quite the opposite. He trusted God with his life and what meant most to him… his family!

Instead of complaining that Evan was taken away from him or what he did not have, instead he thanked God for what he did have. For believers in Christ the certainty of knowing that we will see all believers again in heaven, including our family members who are saved, gives us an unbelievable assurance of hope and joy and ability to live this life as God tells us, "As strangers passing through the Earth on the way to our final destination in Heaven." Living, loving and reaping the fruits of our faith which are joy, love, peace, and happiness. That doesn't mean it's easy; it doesn't mean that tragedies and bad things don't happen to us… it just means that God is with us through them… guiding us… holding us… teaching us… loving us, and that we have the certainty that when our time on Earth is done, we will be with Him in Heaven for all eternity. That is an amazing gift and blessing, and by the way it's available to all. The Word of God clearly says, "All who call upon the name of the Lord will be saved!" Thank you God!

I contrast that with the statement Olivia Newton John made before she passed away this year. The New York post reported it like this:

Olivia Newton-John spoke openly about dying in one of her final interviews — and revealed that she was "sort of looking forward to" being around the energies of the loved ones who passed. The movie star and singer who died in August, opened up last year about how she had been contemplating dying. "I believe there is something that happens. "I hope the energies of the people you love will be there. I've had experiences with spirits". She's hoping, but she doesn't know! Christians know for certain that the Holy Spirit of God is with them in this life and that they will be with God in heaven for all eternity.

I share this with you because she talks about "hoping" and energies of people were there and thinking loved ones will be there and having experience with spirits and spirit life. And I tell you there are other spirits in play that are not godly according to the word of God…I believe many are demonic and following them can land you in hell.

I encourage you to seek the truth of God yourself. Jesus says "I am the way, the truth and the life, the only way to the father is through me" Many have fooled themselves and been let down other paths. The "all roads lead to heaven" saying is a very nice sounding, it's just not true. Just like many people say "the truth always lies in the middle" that's a lot of crap. Sometimes the truth is on one side or the other. Cute sayings and slogans are not the answer. Once again, this year I challenge you to find the truth of God for yourself. If you are not a follower of Jesus, I challenge you to open up the book of John, ask Jesus to reveal himself to you if He is real. He says "if you knock the door will be opened, if you ask you will receive, and if you seek you will find". So if you go to seek God and He doesn't show up you can prove He's a liar. Don't depend on anyone else to tell you…. DON'T! Know the truth yourself for sure!

Many of Hollywood's leading stars, sports athletes, wealthy people, politicians etc. have been led down the path of false religions, rituals and belief. I've yet to meet a man or woman who can tell me I went to meet your God and He didn't show up, unfortunately I met many who won't go look. Try it for a month, five mornings a week ,15 minutes a day open up the gospel of John in the New Testament but before you read to say this one thing "Jesus if your real reveal yourself to me" and then you'll know for yourself if God is real or not!!!

Keep the train rolling. We love you. Have an awesome New Year!

Jack, Beth, Jackson and Talia

December 2023

TIME GONE VOLUME 2

FAMILY UPDATE

Hello Awesome Family and Friends,

We love you all and are so excited to celebrating another holiday season with you. We are praying all of God's best blessings for you, your children and grandchildren, and thank you for being a part of our lives. We believe a man's life is not made up in the abundance of his possessions but is made up in the relationships he has, the love that he or she shares, and the people they got to walk with through this wonderful journey we call life, that we are so privileged to live and experience. On that note thank you for being a part of ours!

WHO'S THE BOSS!

Bruce Springsteen came back on tour this year (after many many years of being off the road… not counting his Broadway solo performances). It was great to again see these legendary life-changing live shows and possibly the greatest experience one could have while living. (Calm down… I said "possibly!")

I saw him three times in February in Florida. Once with Talia in Tampa; it was her first BRUCE concert ever. We had an amazing time. The same week in Orlando I took Jackson... boys' night... It was awesome! The third night I took Beth down to the Hard Rock in Hollywood and we had a beautiful time. It was great to see BRUCE still cranking away as he is almost 75 years old... But once he gets on that stage, he is young again. I know any of these shows could be the last, but will take what we can get... It's been an amazing ride as I saw my first BRUCE show in 1976 and have seen probably 200 shows since then.

A FEW LESSONS GOD TAUGHT ME I THOUGHT YOU MIGHT ENJOY

1. So the other day I was a little frustrated by the concerns of the day, business pressures, thinking about things I want to accomplish that have not been happening as fast as I like. There happens to be a cemetery by my house and I drive by every day since we moved in seven years ago, sometimes multiple times a day. This particular day the Holy Spirit of God spoke to my heart, not audibly but in my spirit, and said, "Look at the cemetery." I said, "God I have

looked at the cemetery, as a matter of fact I have seen it every day for years sometimes multiple times a day. I know it's a cemetery. I see the graves. I get it."

God said, "Let me ask you a question. What do you think matters to these people now?" And I know He was asking me about the things that they were concerned about and worried during their lives… Do they matter now? And of course they do not! Time spent worrying over futile things that they had no control over caused them to waste the time they had rather than enjoying the present. God spoke to my heart again and said, "The only thing that matters to those people now, is what they did for the kingdom of God when they were alive." That's what matters in my life and in your life. I thank God that the Holy Spirit reconfirmed and reminded me of this great truth as God reminds us in Matthew 6:19-21, "Do not lay up for yourselves treasures on earth, where moth and rust destroy and where thieves break in and steal, but lay up for yourselves treasures in heaven, where neither moth nor rust destroys and where thieves do not break in and steal. For where your treasure is, there your heart will be also."

2. Our dog Koda is really a mama's dog as she is Beth's constant companion; she is miserable anytime she is away from Beth for even more than one second. The other day Beth left the house to do some errands and left Koda with me, which she very rarely does, because Koda always wants to be with her. The minute Beth left the house Koda began to cry and wine. She ran around nervously and God spoke to my heart again in the Holy Spirit and He said, "Look at Koda. She's worried, wondering if Beth will ever come back." Because Koda can't see, hear, or speak to Beth, or feel Beth's comforting hand or hear her voice, she's panicked, frustrated, upset, anxious, agitated, and scared! Then God reminded me that of course Beth loves Koda so much. Beth was coming back and Beth had provided for Koda's care while she was gone - she was in good hands, mine!

God reminded me that when I became worried and concerned and anxious about the future, I was behaving just like Koda… that I was not trusting God had provided for me, and just like Koda I was making myself upset, frustrated, and anxious for no reason at all. I was completely provided for and cared for the whole time. I'm reminded of Romans 8:28,

"And we know that in all things God works for the good of those who love him, who have been called according to his purpose." Don't miss this lesson and don't miss this blessing of God. God has us covered! God sees us… God is with us… even if we can't see Him or hear Him or touch Him or feel Him. HE is STILL there. He has provided for us both here on earth and for all eternity in heaven.

3. I heard the best example from a wonderful pastor and mentor of mine, George Cope. When you seal food in a vacuum sealed bag, it takes the air out of the bag and seals it. You see ads for food vacuum sealers on TV. You vacuum seal the food and put it in the freezer to preserve it, so it will last. That's what God has done for us! With Jesus' death on the cross, by His sacrifice, we are preserved forever! We have nothing to worry about. But if that food wasn't preserved in the bag and vacuum sealed it would spoil and rot. If we were not preserved by Christ's blood our place in heaven for all eternity would not be secure; then we too would spoil and rot! But we can rest assured, as believers in Christ, that even when our time on earth is up and we return these earthly bodies that we have rented for our lives here

on earth, we will live in eternity, our spirits forever preserved by God, rejoicing with God, as our place in Heaven is reserved for us by God. This should bring great comfort and peace to every believer. I truly hope that it does. If you don't have that, are you missing out on the kingdom of God here on earth.

4. With all this crazy turmoil we see in the world today, the wars going on in Ukraine and Israel, along with so many other issues, I am reminded that God says, "No one knows the hour or the day" He will return. Our only job is to be faithful! None of what is happening surprises God. God knew before the beginning of the world all of this will happen. It is prophesized and predicted accurately in both the Old and New Testament. Our only job is to be faithful and to be a light in a world of darkness and salt to a tasteless generation. Christians are not supposed to panic. Christians are not supposed to get freaked out about all these things that are happening. We don't have to like them. We don't have to enjoy them. We have to understand God is in control. Again, our job, just like the apostles and disciples and believers of old is just to be faithful to God. To be the love and light of

Christ to the world around us so that people would see our faith and certainty in Jesus and that they would want the same themselves; the peace and joy and salvation and eternal life that comes only from the Lord.

So I want to leave you today with the short letter that was written by Dr. Charles Stanley. This is the last letter he wrote before he passed away this year. A wonderful man of God who lived to be very old and preached right to the end. I believe this letter he sent will speak to your heart and explain a lot of things, especially if you're believer in the Lord. I truly hope it blesses you and inspires you as it did me.

From all of us in Levineland… Happy holidays to you and your family!

Merry Christmas, Happy Hanukkah, Happy New Year and blessings to you all!

To God be the glory!

Love,

Jack Beth Jackson and Talia

2023

CHARLES STANLEY DIED IN APRIL 2023
(This is his last letter)

Have you ever had something stolen from you?

If so, you know the feeling of violation that follows. This happened to me once when someone broke into my car and stole my briefcase. The briefcase itself wasn't a great loss; it was old and worn. And I doubt the thief had any use at all for my Greek New Testament.

But there was something in that old briefcase that was very valuable to me.

It was the Bible my mother had given me. I'd been preaching from it for many years, and it was filled with marked passages and notes on how the Lord had spoken to me through His Word. I was grieved, and for months I felt like I'd lost my best friend.

Someone had intruded into my personal life and stolen the record of my history with the Lord.

There have been times in my life when I've suffered a different kind of loss, and that's the loss of peace.

Sometimes I've been quick to blame the circumstances or other people, even though "assigning blame" was rarely helpful. And there are occasions when I've realized my peace wasn't stolen—I gave it away by focusing on problems, or on people who weren't peaceful themselves.

The truth is, every believer has been given peace with God. We've been reconciled to Him by grace through faith in the Lord's death and resurrection.

And as those united with the Father, we've been given the incomparable peace of Jesus, who said, "My peace I give to you; not as the world gives, do I give to you. Do not let your hearts be troubled, nor fearful" (John 14:27).

Knowing that you have Christ's peace, perhaps you're wondering why there are times when you don't really feel it.

You might find yourself filled with anger, fear, or frustration instead. This side of heaven we'll never have perfect peace in every situation. Some events may cause immediate and justifiable alarm.

But we don't have to let distressing emotions continually hold us in their grip. There is a way to regain our peace, and Paul wrote about it in Philippians 4:6-9.

The first step to regain Christ's peace is to cry out to our heavenly Father.

"Do not be anxious about anything, but in everything by prayer and pleading with thanksgiving let your requests be made known to God" (v. 6). We've all prayed in ways that increase our anxiety by focusing on the situation instead of on the Lord.

Prayer that meditates on scriptural truths about His power and love is a far better approach. The fruit of such prayer will be "the peace of God, which surpasses all comprehension" and guards our hearts and minds (v. 7). The ultimate outcome is an increase in spiritual maturity, because your trust in the Lord has been strengthened.

The second step is to control our thoughts.

This is very important because how we think determines how we feel and what we do. Paul tells us exactly what to focus our minds on—whatever is true, honorable, right, pure, lovely, commendable, excellent, and praiseworthy (v. 8).

Now, if you look at that list, every one of these qualities describes God, His Word, and His ways. When our minds are engaged in thoughts of the Lord, the dark situations that cause us anxiety are diminished.

And Christ's peace fills us, no matter what the circumstances are.

But if we let our thoughts center on things that are not right or good, our trust in God is eroded, and emotions like anger, frustration, and anxiety will dominate us. We find ourselves tossed about like waves in a storm and begin to doubt that God loves us.

We may start to feel that He's abandoned us—even though that's impossible.

Then in desperation we may take matters into our own hands, trying to fix the circumstances to bring stability back into our lives. But God's peace is a gift, not something we can manipulate. And the only way to receive it is to live in obedience to Him.

That brings us to the next step, which is both incredibly simple and a tremendous challenge: Do what God says.

"As for the things you have learned and received and heard and seen in me, practice these things, and the God of peace will be with you" (v. 9). The word practice refers to continuous work.

Each time we read the Bible or hear a biblical sermon, we're responsible for putting the principles we learn into practice. There is no way for a Christian to live in rebellion to God and still have His peace. Sin always brings turmoil.

If you're waiting for the Lord to give you peace by fixing everything in your life that's troublesome, you'll never have it, because His peace has nothing to do with our circumstances.

When Paul wrote his letter to the Philippians, he was unjustly confined in a Roman prison. Yet there is not one word of anger, bitterness, fear, or anxiety in the letter. Instead, he spoke of joy or rejoicing 16 times. What incredible faith!

What's truly remarkable is that the same peace Paul had that surpasses human comprehension is available to you if you're willing to take the steps he's given in his letter. And that is my prayer for you.

Christ has given you His peace. Will you take hold of it today?

Christmas Blessings 2023 - Jack, Beth, Jackson & Talia Levine
"Bless the Lord, O my soul, And forget not all His benefits" Psalm 103:2

December 2024

TIME GONE VOLUME 2

FAMILY UPDATE

Hello Everyone,

Hope you had an awesome year. The Levine family had another wonderful year. Thank you, God, for blessing us and most importantly for you, Lord. Your loves comfort us, saves us, teaches us, and blesses us every day. Thank you for our wonderful family and truly great friends, for a great country and for all the blessings that come living here in America. So, with that said in a heart full of gratitude and thanks, here's the update for the year.

KEEP GOING!

From the "you're not getting older you're getting better department," I got to see Bruce Springsteen a couple of times this year and Bruce has inspired me to preach and speak with fire till the day I die. I get so enthused and excited thinking if Bruce can perform like that at 75 years old with that passion and excitement, I can use that as a reminder to never stop, to continue with a burning desire and passion doing the things that I love. (My favorite being sharing the love, Word, and truth of

God with others.) It was amazing to see Bruce so much older, but he was still the same guy with the same passion. He's given us a great ride and we have aged beautifully together. Thank God we got to share the journey.

We love you all,

Jack, Beth, Jackson and Talia

Some of the next pages, I've written about serious stuff about life that I've been thinking about this year. I hope you will think about about important stuff in your life also

ROMI GONAN PICTURE AND STORY!!!

I don't know why but ever since I saw the picture of the hostages from the Hamas raid on Israel October 7, 2023, I have been praying for this girl (Romi Gonan) daily as she has captured my heart. I don't know why but I cannot shake her or the thought of her out of my mind.

I know there's a lot of hostages and a lot of other people suffering, but to me she represents all the hostages and all the suffering! I pray for her intensely. I can't even imagine what her family is going through or feeling. They are putting on a strong front and speaking out tirelessly on her behalf and on behalf of all hostages and their families. So as I go about my day, occasionally thinking about what bothers me and pisses me off, I think of Romi. This sweet, innocent girl who was attending a concert with friends and had her life changed tragically forever. Then instantly I think of what I have to be grateful for instead of what upsets me.

We know she is one of the captives, we don't know if she is alive… we can only hope and pray. For well over a year I'm just praying that somehow God would use her story to impact, inspire, and rally the world. This does not happen to me often. There only two other times in particular: one with Michael Brewer, a 15 year old back in 2009 in South Florida who was tragically and cruelly set on fire by his classmates, but survived with severe burns all over his body. His life was changed forever by one tragic moment. The day I heard about it, I felt compelled to go to his hospital and pray for him. I stood outside the hospital and prayed for hours and I thank God that he miraculously recovered. Today he is married and has a child of his own.

The other is Evan Leversage, who in 2015 at seven years old was terminally ill and would not live to see Christmas, his favorite holiday. His small hometown in St. George, Ontario decorated the entire town in July to give him the Christmas celebration he would not live to see in December. The town decided if Evan couldn't be there for Christmas then Christmas would be there for Evan! I have written about Evan before many years ago in a holiday letter, but this boy, who I never met, changed my life forever. The story of his life impacted the world as thousands came to the tiny town to fill it up with Christmas cheer, and the world tuned in to see Evan enjoy his Christmas parade while he was alive. I just feel so connected to both Michael and Evan.

I knew God was working at my heart in both of these instances, and now again with Romi Gonan. All we know is on the day she was captured she was shot and when the first hostages were released six months ago it was reported she was alive but had discoloration of her fingers in the hand she was shot in. So please, I ask this holiday season that you will join me in prayer for

Romi, for her release, for safekeeping, for God's hand of protection on her, and somehow for God to provide peace and comfort to her family through this amazingly difficult time. I don't know if it's because she reminds me a little bit of Talia with her infectious smile and similar age, or for some other reason that God has so impressed me with a connection to this girl. I just know God has put her in my heart in a way only He can. Please pray for her! That would be the best Christmas present you could give me.

WHAT DOES THIS REALLY MEAN?

I wanted to share a part of God's Word with you that is often misunderstood and misinterpreted and give you some clarity that I hope will encourage you and inspire you to grow even closer to God.

Proverbs 9:10-12 says, "The fear of the Lord is the beginning of wisdom, and knowledge of the holy one is understanding."

This verse is often misinterpreted as we should fear God! However when you fear something you are afraid of it, and when you're afraid of something you run away from it. That is not the kind of fear the author of Proverbs is talking about in this verse.

You should never fear God. God loves you. He is your Father and only wants what is best for you; He desires to bless you and give you all of His riches and the blessings of an abundant life here on earth and in heaven. But what you should fear is missing out on the blessings of God and that's why the Proverb says the fear of the Lord is the beginning of wisdom. Because if you fear missing out on God's blessings that would inspire you to seek knowledge of God which is understanding. Don't be confused. God is not a mean, uncaring Father just waiting for you to screw up so He can punish you for not being perfect. Quite the opposite. He is forgiving, loving, kind, and loves you for your heart and loves you because you are His and He wants to bless you.

It is like every parent who wants to train up his child in the way that they should go, so they can be blessed, grow strong, and live long, happy, healthy, and productive lives. God desires the same for us. Everything God tells us is for our benefit. We should never fear God. The only time God should be feared is by those who choose to reject Him. They should live in fear that they will miss out on the blessings of God's kingdom and eternity.

The greatest gift anyone could ever receive is to know God, to be counted as one of His, and to be assured their place in eternity is reserved and prepared for them when their time on earth is done, and that God's Holy Spirit is with them, guiding them, and directing them for their time on earth. God never said following Jesus would be easy. He just said it was worth it!

AMERICA TORN APART

We saw what happened in American politics this year. Regardless of which party you were aligned with it was obvious that there was a lot of hatred, anger, and resentment among the different parties. So much so that it divided families, friends, and our country pretty much right down the middle. I personally was so discouraged and disappointed to see this. To see that politics and someone's choice and opinion would be the deciding factor of whether they would be deemed worthy of love and friendship. It surprised me and made me think back to my younger days as a raving Yankee fan. I remember the amazing and treacherous rivalry with the Boston Red Sox. You could say they were the "hated" Boston Red Sox if you were a Yankee fan. Of course those from Boston felt the same way about the Yankees. It was an intense rivalry with much passion on each side.

Yes, there was yelling and shouting and screaming and cheering and refusing to accept the other sides position and accomplishments, regardless of the reality of them, because we were so attuned and in love with our own team. Therefore we would only see blindly our team's greatness, while only acknowledging the other team's faults. But the amazing part of all that was even though the rivalries were intense, WE ALL LOVED BASEBALL! We all loved the game and the rivalry was just that, a rivalry! It was a fun rivalry, even though it was intense. However, Yankee fans would not kill Redsox fans or throw them in jail; they didn't stop talking to friends or family members if they disagreed on which team they chose to root for. No, we just talked and teased and tormented the other guy when his team lost and celebrated when our team won. But at the end of the day we all knew that we all loved baseball! And that's what we had in common, our love for baseball. So it was in our individual rooting of teams that separated us, but it was our love for baseball that united us!

So I was disappointed and amazed to see America ripped apart. To see the hate thrown at those who disagreed with others individual sentiments, to see that it was no longer about America (In this analogy America = baseball). But to see that it became about the individual teams (baseball teams = political parties or candidates). WE ARE ALL AMERICANS! We should all love America; we don't have to like it when our team loses and yes we can certainly have an opinion and cheer for our team, but at the end of the day we need to unite in our common love for America. We are Americans! We are not first Democrats or Republicans or Independents, we are Americans first! Please be joined together. Let this be a season of love, forgiveness, healing, reconciliation, and acknowledgment that we are allowed to have different opinions… on which pizza places are better, on who is the greatest rock 'n' roll band of all time, on the greatest movie or book, and on which party or candidate should be elected to lead our country. But none of these should stifle or snuff out our ability or desire to love each other as individuals from the heart and to remember that we are united together as citizens of this great and amazing country and of this entire world. So perhaps you'll find it in your heart this holiday season to love the Red Sox fans. I know I have. SMILE!!!

2024

COULD HAVE BEEN ME!

So one more earth shattering experience I want to share with you where God spoke to my heart specifically and directly. I was appearing as a character witness for a friend's son who I've known for the last 20 years. Unfortunately my friend's son was involved in a drunk driving accident where he drove drunk and hit another car, and two people died in the car he hit as a result of his drunk driving.

When I was sitting there in the courtroom a few rows behind my buddy whose son was being sentenced, I couldn't help but think that that could be me sitting there with my son Jackson on trial, or it could be my friend Scott and his son Ryan on trial, or it could be my friend Sean and his son Justin who was on trial. It could have been anyone of us, as our kids could have made a stupid mistake or a bad choice and gotten caught up in the system as a consequence of their actions. Then I looked at my friends 32-year-old son and I realized that could be me! That I have made many stupid decisions as a young man… I have driven drunk and stoned, and done things that could easily got me killed or in jail, and there but for the grace of God go I.

But it was when the judge rendered him guilty and sentenced him to life on multiple counts of vehicular manslaughter - and there he was in his suit and tie, and the bailiff slapped the cuffs on him to take him away for life - that the finality and certainty and consequences of sin hit me so hard and dawned on me like never before.

It was in that moment I realized this is what it must be like for non-believers at the very moment they see God on Judgment Day and realize their being led away, taken into the depths of darkness and separated from God for all eternity because of the consequence of their action to deny Jesus. There is also a consequence for believers who do not obey God, although they will not lose God's love or their place in heaven for all eternity, there will be consequences for them here on earth and in heaven. They will miss out on God's blessings and rewards that He has in store for those who are faithful and obedient. I say this not to bum you out but to encourage you to not miss God. All of us want to hear "well done good and faithful servant" when we come face to face with God. We can be certain we will if we believe, listen to, and follow the Lord.

God, I thank you for this living parable you showed me and may I also remember to be grateful for what Jesus did for me on the cross and for the realization that I was once my buddy's kid... we were all my buddy's kid. We are all guilty and deserve to be led away in handcuffs to an eternal prison of condemnation and hell, but thanks be to Jesus who died on the cross for us. He shed His blood to forgive us our sins and give us the door and the keys to the kingdom of life and eternity with God. Thank you, Jesus, for paying the penalty of my sin with your shed blood on the cross. I am so grateful! I love you so much!

GARBAGE DAYS

A close friend of mine shared with me the other day he got news that a 44-year-old friend of his had just found out he had a terminal illness and was days away from dying. So my friend flew up to his hospital bed in Maryland to say a final goodbye. On his deathbed, my friends buddy said this to my friend, "never let one day of your life be a garbage day. Don't throw any day of your life in the garbage. Live every day with joy and happiness and don't let circumstances and things of the world make you miserable so that the day is a garbage day for you."

Those words hit me hard and stayed with me as I vowed to remember to not let any day be a garbage day. That is very consistent with the Word of God which tells us to, "be joyful always, pray continually and give thanks in all circumstances, for this is God's will for us in Christ Jesus." (lst Thessalonians 5:16-18)

I know God speaks to me loudly through His Word but He also often speaks through circumstances and people, as well. I hope you will be inspired and encouraged to not let any day be a garbage day. Life is short. We don't know the time or the end for any of us. Don't waste it! Don't miss God's blessings. For whatever it's worth, I would share with you that true peace, joy, and happiness comes only from the Lord. The things of the world satisfy only momentarily, but still there is a yearning in our heart for continuing, solidified, permanent peace and joy in our lives, not dependent on the circumstances or whimsy of the day's happenings or events. Or by who likes us or who does not. Or over how much money we do or don't have. Or about what job we do or don't have, but instead we are filled with the joy and peace and comfort of the Lord which can never be taken away, which is more valuable than anything ever. We are so grateful for God, for the love that we received accompanied by His peace and comfort which transcends all understanding and His rivers of joy which flow through us... That my friend is what the Christian life is all about! Remember God never said it would be easy... just worth it!

I THINK THE STORE IS CLOSING!

Just a heads up. I think the holiday letters may be coming to an end. For those of you who take time to read them, thank you very much. I appreciate that. I don't feel an obligation to write them as they have always been a joy and I may continue to do it; but don't be surprised if next year it's just a family picture or nothing at all. So if you don't get a letter it just means I've decided to stop writing them. Sometimes some things or seasons in your life come to a close. I prefer to take the Shakespearean attitude, "it is better to have loved and lost than never to have loved at all." I am so grateful for the years of communicating with you and being able to pour out my heart and experiences in these letters. I pray I have not offended anyone in them but have just been transparent about what I believe matters and what the keys to life are.

So in closing here is MY PRAYER FOR ALL OF YOU: it is simply my echoing of the beautiful prayer the apostle Paul prayed for men and women of the church at Corinth and what I believe are three great things every believer should have...

It's 2nd Corinthians 13:14, "May the grace of the Lord Jesus Christ, and the love of God, and the fellowship of the Holy Spirit be with you all."

If you don't have these, THE GRACE OF THE LORD, THE LOVE OF GOD and THE FELLOWSHIP OF THE HOLY SPIRIT... if you are not feeling these, you need to get to know God better. Start by spending time with Him or more time with Him. You do that in prayer and in the reading of God's Word, which is God! (John 1:1, "In the beginning was the Word, and the Word was with God, and the Word was God.")

Lastly, we are leaving you with a holiday gift (on the next page) that I hope will bless you and inspire you. It is Psalm 16.

I would ask that you take time to read it and read it very slowly, savoring each and every word and let

God speak to your heart through it. Then READ IT AGAIN, even slower, savoring each and every word and letting God's Word, live and speak to your heart as you read and hear the truth of God, and see His promises to you. I pray they encourage, inspire, and excite you each and every day of your life. To God be the glory!

Love,

Jack

P.S. Just a reminder, in Jesus' day the cross was not something you would wear; it was something you would bear! And remember problems of this world should not paralyze our minds. They should activate our spirit!

Psalm 16

¹ Keep me safe, my God,
    for in you I take refuge.
² I say to the LORD, "You are my Lord;
    apart from you I have no good thing."
³ I say of the holy people who are in the land,
    "They are the noble ones in whom is all my delight."
⁴ Those who run after other gods will suffer more and
    more.

I will not pour out libations of blood to such gods
  or take up their names on my lips.
5 LORD, you alone are my portion and my cup;
  you make my lot secure.
6 The boundary lines have fallen for me in pleasant places;
  surely I have a delightful inheritance.
7 I will praise the LORD, who counsels me;
  even at night my heart instructs me.
8 I keep my eyes always on the LORD.
  With him at my right hand, I will not be shaken.
9 Therefore my heart is glad and my tongue rejoices;
  my body also will rest secure,
10 because you will not abandon me to the realm of the
  dead, nor will you let your faithful one see decay.
11 You make known to me the path of life;
  you will fill me with joy in your presence,
  with eternal pleasures at your right hand.

FREE BOOKS

Just want to let you know God has put it on my heart to make available free e-book copies of all my books this holiday season. I hope they will be a blessing to those searching for a closer walk with God as well as those struggling with addiction. There are some God books and some Overcoming Addiction books.

Please feel free to pass this link on to anyone you know and post on social media as well. They can download any (and as many) of my books as they like for free as an e-book download.

LINK TO JACKS FREE BOOKS:

JackAlanLevine.com/ebooks

www.ingramcontent.com/pod-product-compliance
Lightning Source LLC
Chambersburg PA
CBHW060357080526
44583CB00012B/363